Trust & Betrayal in the Workplace

Building Effective Relationships in Your Organization

Dennis S. Reina & Michelle L. Reina

Berrett–Koehler Publishers, Inc.
San Francisco

Berrett-Koehler Publishers, Inc.
450 Sansome Street, Suite 1200, San Francisco, CA 94111-3320
Tel: (415) 288-0260; Fax: (415) 362-2512; www.bkconnection.com

ORDERING INFORMATION

Quantity sales. Special discounts are available on quantity purchases by corporations, associations, and others. For details, contact the "Special Sales Department" at the Berrett-Koehler address above.

Individual sales. Berrett-Koehler publications are available through most bookstores. They can also be ordered direct from Berrett-Koehler: Tel: (800) 929-2929; Fax: (802) 864-7626; www.bkconnection.com

Orders for college textbook/course adoption use.
Please contact Berrett-Koehler: Tel: (800) 929-2929; Fax: (802) 864-7626.

Orders by U.S. trade bookstores and wholesalers. Please contact Publishers Group West, 1700 Fourth Street, Berkeley, CA 94710
Tel: (510) 528-1444; Fax (510) 528-3444.

Printed in the United States of America

Printed on acid-free and recycled paper that is composed of 50% recovered fiber, including 10% post consumer waste).

Library of Congress Cataloging-in-Publication Data

Reina, Michelle, 1958–
    Trust and betrayal in the workplace : building effective
relationships in your organization / Michelle and Dennis Reina.
       p. cm.
    Includes bibliographical references and index.
    ISBN 1-57675-070-1 (alk. paper)
    1. Organizational behavior.   2. Trust.   3. Interpersonal
relations.   4. Organizational effectiveness.   5. Work environment.
6. Psychology, Industrial.   I. Reina, Dennis, 1950– .   II. Title.
III. Title: Trust and betrayal in the workplace.
HD58.7.R4388   1999
158.7—dc21

                                             99-41538
                                             CIP

First Edition
05 04 03 02 01 00 99 10 9 8 7 6 5 4 3 2 1

Cover design: Stacey Hood
Interior design and production: Jonathan Peck, Dovetail Publishing Services

For our children, Patrick and William,

and our godchildren, Timothy and Julia,

Who open our hearts

And nurture our capacity to trust

CONTENTS

PREFACE

This book is about trust: the power when it exists, the problems when it doesn't, and the pain when it is betrayed. Our purpose in writing this book is to help people at all levels of the organization create, support, and rebuild trust in themselves and within their organizations.

This book is about creating more productive and rewarding work environments for all—where work relationships are built on trust, are infused with spirit, and inspire leaders and employees alike. The principles and practices, tools and techniques offered in *Trust & Betrayal in the Workplace* apply to anyone, in any kind of relationship and in any kind of setting.

Today more than ever, there is a need for trust in the workplace. People are in pain, and organizations are hurting. After years of constant change—years of downsizing, restructuring, and reengineering or of upsizing, mergers, and growth—trust among people at every level in the organization is at an all-time low.

You may have personally felt the pain of a breach of trust or even a betrayal during the course of your working career. People you work with may have misread your intentions when you honestly felt you were acting in the best interests of the organization. You may have been accused of not "walking your talk" or been disappointed when others fell similarly short.

Unmet expectations, disappointments, broken trust, and betrayals aren't restricted to big events like restructurings and downsizings. They crop up every day on the job. Leaders are beginning to realize that people's trust and commitment to the organization affect their performance. We use the term *leaders* in a broad sense, referring to all individuals who demonstrate leadership behaviors at all levels of responsibility.

Trust takes time to develop; it is easy to lose and hard to regain. It is a fragile yet indispensable element in any relationship. By first trusting in themselves and others, it is possible for leaders to develop caring, genuine relationships and build trust with their people.

WHO SHOULD READ THIS BOOK

This book is designed to help anyone who has the desire to cultivate trusting relationships with the people with whom they work. Our focus is on managers and leaders who seek to help people at all levels who have lost trust in and feel betrayed by the organizations for which they work. These leaders face what may seem like an overwhelming task of rebuilding trust with people and may not be sure how to go about it. This book is designed to help them and those they turn to for support, such as human resource and organizational development professionals.

We explore behaviors that build trusting relationships and behaviors that contribute to betrayal. *Trust & Betrayal in the Workplace* will help people understand the complex dynamics of trust and betrayal. It serves as a comprehensive reference and practical guide to building trust between individuals, within teams, and throughout organizations.

OVERVIEW OF THE BOOK

Understanding the complexity of trust and betrayal is challenging work. The topic of trust is emotionally charged and means different things to different people. We developed the Reina Trust & Betrayal Model to increase your awareness of the dynamics of trust and betrayal and to provide a shared understanding and a common language to help you discuss trust-related issues, take action on trust-related matters, and create and maintain healthy levels of trust in your organization. The model provides the framework for this book. It is built layer by layer, with figures illustrating the important components that contribute to trust between people, within teams, and throughout organizations at each step.

The book has three parts. Part I provides a conceptual framework for understanding the dynamics of trust and betrayal in work relationships.

In Chapter 1, we examine the pain and price when trust is low or does not exist and the payoff when it does. We define *trust* and *betrayal* and introduce the Reina Trust & Betrayal Model.

In Chapter 2, we start with the first figure of the model, *capacity for trust*. We examine the two main dimensions of this capacity: trusting oneself and trusting others and the influence of one's capacity for trust on one's perceptions and beliefs. The remaining chapters contribute to building the model.

In Chapter 3, we identify four capacity-for-trust scales and set out specific steps and exercises for using them to increase one's capacity for trust.

In Chapter 4, we explore the nature of betrayal, its effect on one's capacity for trust, and the ways in which people betray themselves and others in the workplace. In Chapter 5, we set forth seven steps for overcoming betrayal and examine what you as an individual can do to "get yourself off the floor" after you have been betrayed. This chapter deals with hands-on, practical things people can do to get some help in dealing with their pain.

In Part II, we focus on the development of *transactional trust* between people in organizations. In Chapters 6, 7, and 8, we examine the three types of transactional trust—*contractual, communication, and competence trust*—detailing what they are and behaviors people can use to develop them.

Chapters 9 and 10 deal with the issues of trust at the team and organizational levels, respectively. In Chapter 9, we examine principles and practices related to building trust at the team or group level. We talk about team members' concerns, anxieties, and fears regarding trust. We explore ways to create an open atmosphere where blame is eliminated and learning is stressed. In Chapter 10, we investigate issues and practices related to building trust at the organizational level. We explore the steps that you can take to help your organization heal and move out of betrayal toward trust.

In Part III, we show how the model can serve as a developmental tool you can use to understand the dynamics of trust and betrayal and move your organization toward the highest form of trust, *transformative trust*.

In the final chapter, we examine the power of transformative trust in organizations: what it is, how it works, and how you can create it. We review the four core characteristics that contribute to creating transformative trust: conviction, courage, compassion, and community.

At the end of each chapter is a section headed "Ideas in Action" in which we provide reflective questions to aid understanding and self-discovery and application exercises that allow you to use the material to develop your capacity to trust as an individual and improve the capacity of trust in others.

DEVELOPMENT OF THIS BOOK

Trust & Betrayal in the Workplace is the product of our twenty-five years of collective experience working with people in a variety of ways. We have had the privilege of working internally, as managers and human resource professionals, as well as externally, as organizational consultants serving a broad range of industries. We have seen how pervasive the lack of trust is in organizations and how it interferes with people's abilities to contribute fully to their organizations. We have worked extensively with leaders grappling with the need to rebuild trust with their employees. Through our efforts to help others understand, we felt compelled to develop a deeper understanding ourselves.

The roots of this book were planted a number of years ago with Dennis's doctoral dissertation on the development of trust in work teams. We then conducted additional research specifically for this book. We interviewed 125 organizational leaders, managers, supervisors, and human resource and organizational development professionals from sixty-seven different organizations in the United States and Canada.

Our research included organizations in the manufacturing, health care, aerospace, higher education, chemical, petroleum, pharmaceuticals, telecommunications, computer and electronics, banking, hotel and resort, social services, engineering, accounting, law, food, and utilities industries, as well as the federal and state governments. The average interview lasted two and one-half hours. People opened their hearts to us and shared their experiences. Many of the interviewees expressed relief at being at last able to share thoughts, concerns, and feelings about the types of trusting relationships they desired that they were not at liberty to express openly with their colleagues at work. The stories and quotes in the book come from the actual experiences of our research interviewees and our clients. The names and locations of individuals and organizations have been changed to maintain confidentiality.

As an outgrowth of our research, we developed the Reina Trust & Betrayal Model, which became a foundation for workshops, learning guides, and instruments that measure trust on the individual, team, and organization levels. Our workshops and instruments further developed our thinking and provided us with a deeper understanding of trust and betrayal.

Our interest in trust is passionate. We believe that all human beings deserve to trust in themselves and to feel safe to trust in others. We wrote this book to that end.

Stowe, Vermont   Dennis S. Reina
July 1999   Michelle L. Reina

ACKNOWLEDGMENTS

The writing of this book has truly been a privileged experience. The process has provided us with an opportunity to learn to listen to our inner voice and speak from our minds and hearts in an integrated fashion. Because we have been working with and writing about a topic, trust, that is so dear to us, it was important that we be true to ourselves in what we wrote and how we wrote it. We have been blessed to be surrounded by a circle of loving people who have trusted in us, trusted in the contribution this book will make to others, and remained supportive throughout this process.

There were long stretches when the writing of this book was all-consuming and we were not available to the world outside our offices. Our sons, Patrick and William, have stood by us, cheered us on, cooked for us, and demonstrated patience and understanding well beyond their years. Yes, sweethearts, the book is done! And we love you with all our hearts.

Our families have provided a steady stream of encouragement and faith in us and what we might bring to others. They have graciously understood our need for isolation and therefore long periods of silence.

Valerie Barth, senior editor with Berrett-Koehler, shared our vision for this book when it consisted of a two-page outline: "This is a book that needs to be written," she told us, "and you are the ones to write it." Thank you for your trust in us.

Richard Weaver provided thoughtful guidance throughout the entire development of this book, from first outline through completion. Richard, you have given far beyond what we could have hoped for from a friend. What we have shared together has been "transformative."

Our friends John Shorb, Dana Morris-Jones, Debbie Burke, Chris Robbins, Betty Myers, and MB McDonald provided insightful feedback on the first draft of the manuscript that helped develop our thinking further and bring shape to the final manuscript.

Suggestions for improvement from Berrett-Koehler reviewers Kendra Armer, Andrea Markowitz, Sara Jane Hope, and Paul Wright helped take our work to a higher level.

Kristen Frantz, Berrett-Koehler staffer, has been a real champion and a kindred spirit. In Kristen we have found a new and trusted friend.

We have learned from more people in our work with organizations than it is possible to name. From them we have learned the power of trust and the hope for future relationships in organizations. We are particularly grateful to all the individuals who so willingly shared their experiences and views and gave of themselves during our research. You have all been our teachers.

Rich discussions with Art Lerner, Richard Hossack, and David Sibbett were inspirational and contributed to the development of the Reina Trust & Betrayal Model.

Linda Tobey and Katrina Burrus were there for us throughout the long haul and lifted our spirits at just the right times.

Jeffrey Douglas helped us to further discover our voice and to honor it. Our unfolding relationship has been a gift.

Stacey Hood, Barbara Grant, Kathy Leith, and Norma Farnsworth, members of the Chagnon & Reina Associates team, have been especially valuable. Stacey is the creative gem who brought our model to life through the use of graphics and design. Barbara has provided support above and beyond the call of duty and has shared in the unfolding spirit of this book. Kathy and Norma provided a stable force in the other aspects of our life that allowed us to focus. The four of you have embraced our vision and helped bring it to fruition. Thank you.

Finally, we would like to acknowledge the process of life that has brought the two of us together and has provided us with an opportunity to make a contribution to the development of trust in the workplace.

UNDERSTANDING TRUST AND BETRAYAL

The dynamics of trust and betrayal in the workplace are complex. That is the reason people have difficulty understanding them, much less being able to deal with them. In Part I, we define what trust and betrayal are and introduce the Reina Trust & Betrayal Model to help you understand and manage their multiple dynamics.

1

THE NEED FOR TRUST

The agony of betrayal involves the sudden tearing of
the delicate fabric of trust that has united us.
JOHN AMODEO

In this chapter, you will learn about:

- The pain of betrayal
- Why leaders need to deal with betrayal
- The payoff of building trust
- Understanding trust and betrayal

"I can't believe this is happening to me!" Margie looked around the room. It felt more like a funeral parlor than the hospital where she had worked since John F. Kennedy was in the White House. "Laid off? It can't be true! One hundred twenty-four of us out the door and we didn't have any warning. Even the people who are staying are angry. Do they really believe that they can maintain a high standard of patient care after this?" After coming to work in the same place for over thirty-five years, at this moment Margie had no idea what she was going to do next. She felt devastated. She felt betrayed.

"Stick my neck out again? No way!" thought Harry, VP of operations. The CEO of a utility company had said to his executive team,

3

*"From now on, I would like to have team involvement in the key deci-
sions that affect this company." Yet the CEO continued to make key
decisions unilaterally. When Harry tried diplomatically to call this
inconsistency to the CEO's attention, Harry was shocked at the
response: he was publicly discredited, his workload was increased, his
deadlines were shortened, and a long overdue raise was eliminated. "I
thought I had a good relationship with our CEO. I knew he wouldn't
like what I was saying, but I never thought he would attack me personally for saying it. I thought we were supposed to be a team, and look at
what happened to me!" Harry felt bitterly betrayed. "And it is not just
me. I see that no one else is going to risk saying anything other than
'yes sir.'"*

THE PAIN OF BETRAYAL

You may have personally felt the pain of being in similar situations or wit-
nessed others going through such agonizing episodes during the course
of your working career. You may have been misunderstood by your boss,
your colleagues, or your employees in a way that led them to think less of
you or not trust you as much. Or maybe a trusted coworker with whom
you shared sensitive information in confidence later violated your trust.
Or maybe a peer with whom you have been working closely on a project
stole the credit you deserved and got the promotion you felt you earned.
Though these betrayals range on a continuum from small to huge, each
one of them affects us deeply, whether we are willing to admit it or not.

   You are not alone. These scenarios are reflective of the types of
betrayals that take place in corporate America every day. As a result of situations like these, the trust gap in the workplace is widening. Leaders,
navigating the change within their organizations, are losing credibility
with their employees. They are "losing their employees' loyalty, their trust
and their commitment—the very intangibles that keep corporate ships
seaworthy."[1] Leaders are losing credibility in their organizations.

   And feelings of betrayal in the workplace are not limited to layoffs.
Although downsizing is often blamed for the breach, poor leadership
behaviors are many times the real culprits. For example, both not shar-

ing information and not involving others in decisions that affect their lives provoke feelings of betrayal.

Despite the fact that many employees feel betrayed by leadership, leaders are not the sole source of betrayal in the workplace. Leaders can feel betrayed by the people they supervise.

Tina, a manager in a federal government agency, had total confidence in Paul. She gave him a lot of latitude to do his job but felt that he took advantage of her trust in him. He perpetually used government time to satisfy personal needs without concern for the impact of his absence on workflow and coworkers. When questioned directly by Tina about his behavior, he lied to her in an attempt to cover up his deception. Tina felt betrayed. "I have to work with him, but how can I ever trust him again?"

As Tina learned, betrayal does not flow in only one direction, from managers to the people they supervise. Feelings of betrayal are experienced in all types of workplace relationships. In fact, people at all levels of organizations are feeling betrayed. It happens every day on the job—whether it is between leaders and employees or among employees. When people's expectations are not met, when they feel taken advantage of, when they are excluded from decisions that affect their jobs and their lives, when their creativity is suppressed, they feel betrayed and feel the pain associated with that betrayal.

Some betrayals are driven by fear or even greed. They are fed by people not keeping their agreements or misleading coworkers to further their own ends. As one concerned employee pointed out, "When we get double-crossed by our closest coworkers, the dagger of betrayal stabs us most deeply." And no matter how many times we face betrayal, it is always painful and shocking; it is not something we ever get used to.[2]

Some forms of betrayal may seem harmless and insignificant yet can lead to more serious hurts and account for much of the pain and resignation employees feel toward their bosses, each other, and their companies. Not keeping one's word, talking behind someone's back, not sharing pertinent information or resources, not respecting other people's skills and talents or judgment—these are examples of everyday betrayals.

WHY LEADERS NEED TO DEAL WITH BETRAYAL

Betrayal is systemic: it affects the whole system. Like a migraine headache, it is not just your head that is affected by the pain but your whole body. Betrayal, like a migraine headache, is energy-depleting and can shut down a whole system. If you have a migraine, you can't work. If you feel betrayed, you may continue to show up at work, but you will not be very effective while brooding about your feelings.

Employees who value openness and honesty often become discouraged attempting to work in an atmosphere polluted by distrust. The greater the employees' commitment toward and involvement in their jobs and their company, the greater the betrayal they feel. Over time, employees become cynical from the cumulative effect of these bruising betrayals and lose confidence in their organizations. Employees reach the point where they *expect* to be betrayed.

Betrayal is an experience determined by the betrayed. Sometimes a person feels betrayed even when the betrayer has made an effort to minimize the negative effects on people and the organization.

Joe, manager of a manufacturing plant in the Northeast, tries to do what is right for the company and what is good for his people. Three years ago, corporate headquarters ordered a major restructuring of his plant. Joe had to consolidate five departments and lay off people. Though the total number of people to be let go was only seventeen, the fear, anxiety, and turmoil their termination created throughout the plant was tremendous. Joe knew of the pending change months before he took action. He kept the information to himself, thinking it would minimize the negative impact. However, when the news hit the shop floor, the employees were shocked and angered. "Why weren't we informed? Why didn't they ask us what we thought? We might have had a better solution!" Three years have passed, and the negative feelings still linger; in some cases, they have gotten worse. Employees no longer trust Joe, his managers, or the company. They are skeptical of any improvements management tries to make. Many employees feel they gave their loyalty to the company and were betrayed.

Haven't most people, much to their chagrin, found their actions and their words interpreted differently from the way they were intended? They may feel bad that they inadvertently caused others pain, but they did the best they felt they could.

We know that Joe is not alone in this struggle. During the course of our work and our research, many leaders, from the CEO level to supervisors on the shop floor, shared with us their thoughts, concerns, and feelings—feelings they did not feel safe enough to express openly in their work environments. Leaders and employees alike expressed fears about anticipated future changes and a lack of trust in their companies, their bosses, their peers, and their employees.

We have seen countless company change efforts, teams, and projects fail because of a lack of trust in the people initiating the change. We have seen vice presidents undermine each other, managers hide their opinions, and employees sabotage projects because they did not trust each other.

Due to sweeping changes taking place at all corporate levels around the globe, individuals and organizations are increasingly vulnerable to experiencing betrayal. It is important that we all be alert to the conditions that foster trust and those that trigger its opposite. With change comes opportunity but also uncertainty, fear, and anxiety. Nowadays, people do not trust their future, their organizations, or themselves as they did in the past. And based on the past ten years of restructurings, mergers, and acquisitions, organizational changes over the next ten years will influence people even more.

To thrive in the new global economy, company leaders and managers must recognize the need to create open and flexible organizations that are able to adapt to the rapidly changing conditions of the marketplace. Flexibility requires a force of workers that trust their leaders, one another, and themselves. It requires that people explore new ways of doing things. It requires taking risks. Trust in one's leaders, coworkers, and oneself makes taking risks possible. People who trust are more willing to let go of what was and try something new.

The business dynamics surrounding trust create a paradoxical challenge. Leaders are called on to build open and flexible organizations that are competitive and at the same time to develop a healthy level of employee trust in increasingly distrustful working environments. The disappearance of the old employment contract, downsizing, and company growth come at a high cost in employee loyalty and trust. Unfortunately, the cost is not short-term; it may continue covertly to undermine organizations for many years. Low trust impedes organizational leaders from achieving objectives. Low trust eats away at the bottom line and the overall health of the organization.

Of crucial importance is not *what* change happens but rather *how* change happens. When leaders twist the truth or spin the facts, employees feel betrayed and fear the results. When people work in fear, they are guarded and calculating in their actions. The best they have to offer is no longer available. They function in a constricted manner, cut off from their creativity and their intuition, afraid of making the "wrong move" or saying the "wrong thing." This greatly affects information and resource sharing, problem solving, and decision making.

Employees' desire for stability and security places leaders today in a real bind. They cannot guarantee their employees lifetime or even long-term employment. Understandably, employees are unwilling to commit all of their energy, skill, and talent to a company unwilling to commit to them. As Mary, a once dedicated and hardworking employee, said, "I used to work for this company; now I just work for myself." The old informal contract is gone, and often there is no new one to take its place. The result is tentative relationships with low trust and commitment. Many of the best employees voluntarily take early retirement or find new jobs because they are fed up with what is going on and jump at the chance to change employers.

THE PAYOFF OF BUILDING TRUST

The goal of business is not to create trust per se. However, business is conducted via relationships, and trust is the foundation of relationships. Trust should be a by-product of the decisions and actions of people carrying out the business of their organizations. Directly and indirectly, trust is related to individual, group, and overall organizational performance.

Higher trust within an organization increases creativity and critical thinking, necessary factors for flexible and adaptive work environments.

When leaders create trusting working environments, people are safe to challenge the system and perform beyond expectations. Employees feel more freedom to express their creative ideas. They are more willing to takes risks, admit mistakes, and learn from those mistakes.

Julie, a customer service manager of a telecommunications firm, thought she was operating with the best interest of the company in mind. Yet at a meeting of her management team the day before, Julie's boss did not support her. In fact, he belittled her with his unfounded remarks. Julie was upset, but said nothing to her boss in her defense. After the meeting, she quickly left the room feeling quite defeated.

The next day Julie took a risk. She knew she could be fired for speaking up. Yet she also knew she had to do something and do it soon! After a sleepless night worrying, Julie walked into her boss's office and asked if they could talk. She told her side of the story: that she felt misunderstood and betrayed by her boss's comments and actions the day before. She felt that her boss's comments were not justified. The two of them talked the situation through. The boss admitted the mistake he made, and Julie took responsibility for her part. Both talked about what they would do to prevent misunderstanding in the future. Julie and her boss were able to restore trust and confidence in each other and in their relationship.

In working through the issues and restoring trust in her relationship with her boss, Julie was able to refocus on accomplishing the tasks of her job, not worrying about whether she had one. Taking the time to build and maintain trust in the workplace allows employees to focus their energies on what they are there to do and want to do. As a result, suggestions for product and process improvements proliferate, and productivity increases as employees develop a sense of pride and ownership in their jobs and meaning in their work.

Trust-inspiring work environments are liberating. When employees feel good about the people they are working with and the company they are working for, they enjoy coming to work and generally work harder at their jobs, giving more of themselves—accepting challenges and seeing them as opportunities.

UNDERSTANDING TRUST AND BETRAYAL

Trust in the workplace is difficult for many people to understand because of its complexity. Trust means different things to different people. For some people, it means keeping agreements—formal or informal, written or unwritten. For others, it means open communication between individuals. For still others, it means reliance on capabilities or competence.

The first step in understanding trust is to start with a common definition so that everyone is "on the same page." We offer the following components in building a definition of trust in the workplace.

The Four C's of Trust

- *Capacity for Trust:* Our readiness to trust
- *Contractual Trust:* Trust of character
- *Communication Trust:* Trust of disclosure
- *Competence Trust:* Trust of capability

Thus *trust* is a relationship of mutual confidence in contractual performance, honest communication, expected competence, and a capacity for unguarded interaction.

Betrayal is an intentional or unintentional breach of trust or the perception of a breach of trust. An intentional betrayal is a self-serving action done with the purpose of hurting, damaging, or harming another person. An unintentional betrayal is the by-product of another person's self-serving action that results in people being hurt, damaged, or harmed.

The Reina Trust & Betrayal Model illustrates the complex nature of trust and betrayal in work relationships in a simplified way. It is built layer by layer, with each figure illustrating the important components that contribute to trust between people, within teams, and throughout organizations. The model also provides the framework for the remainder of this book. Each component will be explained in depth in the following chapters.

IDEAS IN ACTION

Here we examine what leaders can do to understand trust and betrayal in the workplace.

Questions to Consider

The first step of any healing process is awareness. Reflect on the following questions, and record your thoughts in a journal.

1. What is your definition of trust?
2. What is your definition of betrayal?
3. In what ways and under what circumstances have you experienced betrayal in your personal or work life? How did these experiences of betrayal affect the ways you trusted yourself and others?
4. Describe a betrayal you observed in your work setting. What consequences did you observe arising from those betrayals?
5. Describe a situation in which trust was rebuilt after a betrayal. What difference did that rebuilding of trust make?

2

UNDERSTANDING OUR CAPACITY FOR TRUST

Trust that still, small voice that says,
"This might work and I'll try it."
DIANE MARIECHILD

In this chapter, you will learn about:

- The nature of our capacity for trust
- Trusting ourselves
- Trusting others
- The impact of our capacity for trust on our perceptions and our beliefs
- How our capacity for trust develops

THE NATURE OF OUR CAPACITY FOR TRUST

Fundamental to understanding trust is understanding our capacity for trust. Our capacity for trust is our readiness to trust ourselves and others (see Figure 1). When we trust ourselves, we see ourselves as reliable and dependable to others. When we trust others, we feel we can rely on their judgment, and we have confidence in them. Our capacity for trust influences our perceptions and our beliefs. It also involves managing our

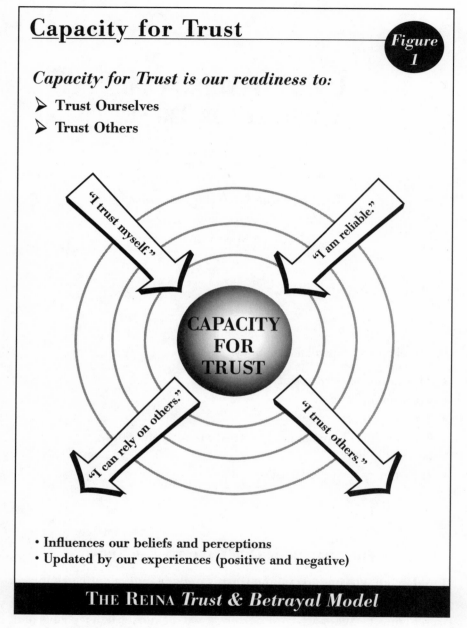

Capacity for Trust

Figure 1

Capacity for Trust is our readiness to:

➤ **Trust Ourselves**
➤ **Trust Others**

"I trust myself."

"I am reliable."

CAPACITY FOR TRUST

"I can rely on others."

"I trust others."

- **Influences our beliefs and perceptions**
- **Updated by our experiences (positive and negative)**

THE REINA *Trust & Betrayal Model*

Figure 1 The Capacity for Trust

expectations of ourselves and others. Our capacity for trust expands or contracts, depending on our experiences, positive or negative. To explore this definition further, we will look at each dimension separately.

TRUSTING OURSELVES

Trust in ourselves is our tendency to view ourselves as dependable and reliable in fulfilling our expectations of ourselves and the expectations others have of us. Our sense of who we are, our identity, and feedback from others all affect the degree to which we trust ourselves.

Trust in ourselves is indispensable to a sense of self and self-esteem. It is considered the "glue of our individual experience" that holds together our sense of who we are (our identity) and how we deal with others and our world. When we have a high level of trust in ourselves, we have a strong sense of confidence. Trust in ourselves enables us to deal with ambiguous situations and uncertainty in our jobs. People who have a healthy level of trust and confidence in themselves tend to be trusted more by others than those who have low trust in themselves.

Trust in ourselves may be monitored by listening to the voice within. This is the voice within you that just asked, "What voice?" That same voice asks such questions as "Can I do this?" "Do I believe I have what it takes to achieve this goal?" "Am I capable of learning this new program?" "Will I get this project done on time?" "Am I able to live up to the new bosses' expectations of me?"

Each of us has asked these questions of ourselves at one time or another during our working lives. You can be assured that these are questions employees are asking themselves. Although we may not answer these questions consciously, we answer them daily through our actions. Our actions affect our sense of self-worth.

Our capacity to trust directly affects our attitude toward taking risks and trying new things. We know that an athlete is capable of accomplishing only what he or she believes is possible. For example, if a pole vaulter does not believe that he is capable of clearing eighteen feet, the chances are pretty slim that he will achieve that objective.[1] Likewise, at work, an employee may be given a task to complete on a short deadline.

If she simply assumes, without honestly assessing the task requirements, that there's no way she is going to be able to complete it on time, she will prove herself right and fail to get the job done.

TRUSTING OTHERS

Trust in others is our tendency to view others as dependable and reliable in fulfilling our expectations. In forming our trust in others, our voice may ask: "Can I really trust my coworkers?" "Are they able to do what it takes when the chips are down?" "Can I trust them to do their part to get this project completed and to the customer on time?"

Our capacity to trust in others is critical to our work relationships. It is the force that holds a relationship together. When we have a high capacity to trust others, we are more willing and able to work in a fluid fashion. We share information and depend on others. Our capacity to trust others enables us to loosen the necessity to control people in making sure a job gets done. Leaders who are more trusting in others are more trusted by others in return. Leaders who have a high capacity for trust are willing to trust another person until they have clear evidence that he or she can't be trusted. A leader with a low capacity for trust may not be willing to trust another person unless there is clear evidence that the person can be trusted.[2]

Our capacity to trust others influences performance. Healthy working relationships are based on trust, not legal contracts or money-back guarantees. We know that trust is a reciprocal process: trust begets trust. Generally speaking, the more we give, the more we get. Mutual trusting relationships grow the more we share information *(Communication Trust)*, keep agreements *(Contractual Trust)*, and respect people's abilities *(Competence Trust)*.

A higher capacity to trust others enables us to take risks. Risk taking means being willing and able to deal with uncertainty and ambiguity, take calculated chances, and share pertinent information, including our inner thoughts and feelings when appropriate. Though there are no guarantees in any relationship, personal or professional, it is easier to risk trusting others when we have trust in ourselves.

IMPACT ON OUR PERCEPTIONS

"Is the glass half empty or half full?" Our capacity to trust influences our perceptions. Perceptions are our observations or comprehension of the world. They are what we believe through our own eyes to be true at the moment.

It has often been said that "perception equals reality." Fortunately or unfortunately, this is especially true when it comes to the role of trust in relationships at work. It is helpful for leaders, in particular, to be aware of this important fact. Whether employees believe a leader or not depends on their perception of the leader's trustworthiness. Our perceptions of the other person's intentions and competence determine trust.[3]

IMPACT ON OUR BELIEFS

"Is the world a safe place?" Our capacity to trust determines whether we believe things will work out for the best in the end.[4] This relates to our general expectations in life. Most of these expectations are commonplace, taken-for-granted social and moral behaviors that we operate by and generally do not think much about. Stopping at red lights and pulling over for a flashing ambulance are examples.

In organizations, since our capacity for trust influences our beliefs, people "bring themselves to work" from a continuum of perspectives. At one end of the continuum is entitlement; at the other is contribution. Those who come from entitlement look at the world through the lens of scarcity. These are the people who feel that the company and the world owe them a living. In relationships at work, they wait for something good to happen before they are willing to acknowledge another person or before they are willing to give trust.

But there are also people in organizations who come from a place of contribution. They look at the world through the lens of abundance. They are willing to give to others first while not worrying about what they are getting in return. Because of their positive outlook, sense of appreciation, and trust in others, they attract more things to appreciate and trust in their relationships. These folks are like gardeners, cultivating their relationships and nurturing them with trust.

Highly successful leaders are like gardeners cultivating relationships with employees and nurturing them with trust. As leaders develop trusting relationships, they are better able to coach employees and move them along the continuum from entitlement toward contribution.

HOW OUR CAPACITY FOR TRUST DEVELOPS

According to developmental psychologists, we start developing our capacity for trust from the time we are born. The first two years of life are especially critical to this development. During the first year, through the loving care of primary caregivers, we develop our fundamental capacity to trust others.[5] From our first year's experience, we develop our perceptions and beliefs about people—the degree to which we perceive them as being basically good and trustworthy or bad and untrustworthy.[6]

During the second year of life, as we develop mentally and physically and start to become more self-reliant, we learn to trust ourselves. As we develop muscle coordination and become more mobile, we also become more aware of ourselves as individuals separate from our parents. (If you are a parent, you may well remember your children's going through the "terrible twos," learning to say "no" and getting into everything.) From this experience, we develop confidence in ourselves, which influences our willingness to take risks and trust in our competence to resolve problems and overcome difficult situations.

As one continues to grow through adolescence and into adulthood, the basis for trusting oneself and others—the capacity for trust—develops from the concrete to the abstract, from simple to complex: "I trust it because I can see it" to "If I do something for you, will you do something for me?" to "You have my word—you can depend on me, no matter what!"

Though we may experience predictable changes over the course of our lives, the changes do not necessarily occur in successive or linear stages, one replacing another. The developmental changes we experience may remain fully functioning and active within us throughout our lives.[7]

IDEAS IN ACTION

Here we examine what leaders can do to comprehend and expand their capacity for trust. The questions and exercises may also be used by a leader or a facilitator to coach other individuals or a team.

Questions to Consider

Reflect on the following questions, and record your thoughts. If you are working with a team, have team members share their thoughts. Discuss how attitude toward trust affects how people on your team or in your organization relate to one another and how work gets done.

1. Do you trust yourself? In what types of situations can you answer yes? In what situations is the answer no? In what ways do you consider yourself reliable? In what ways do you feel you are unreliable?

2. Do you trust others? Again, in what situations can you say yes and in which ones no? What do you look for when considering whether another person is trustworthy?

3. Do you tend to assume that others can be trusted until proved otherwise, or do you wait for people to prove they are trustworthy? How does this tendency, one way or the other, affect your personal and work relationships?

Application Exercises

These activities are intended to give you an opportunity to apply the material to develop your capacity to trust or to assist you in helping others do so.

A. Create what you want through affirmations. Affirmations are positive statements in the present tense that affirm what we want to create in our lives, for example: "I trust myself"; "I am capable of doing what it takes to get the job done." Before anything can materialize in the physical world, it is first created in the cognitive or idea world. Repeating affirmations on a daily basis creates the ideas to help align the needed actions to achieve the desired results.

   B. Think about a situation you want to change or create in your life (for example, "I would like to be less controlling and more trusting of myself and others").

1. Write affirmations that reflect changes you wish to make. Write them as though they are already happening (for example, "I have full trust in myself," "I am trusting of others"). Write as many as you can think of that relate to the goal or condition you want to achieve.
2. Pick the one or two that seem most appropriate for achieving your desired state. Write them repeatedly on a sheet of paper.
3. Transfer your affirmations to Post-it notes and place them in prominent places where you can see them. Repeat them out loud to yourself at least three times a day.
4. Practice them every day for at least three weeks. (Experience shows it takes twenty-one consecutive days of practice for a behavior to become a habit.)

   The consistent expression of affirmations is self-validating. Voicing our desired results on a daily basis helps us align our actions to achieve our goals and expand our capacity for trust.

3

THE FOUR CAPACITY FOR TRUST SCALES

*Trust in yourself. Your perceptions are far
more accurate than you are willing to believe.*
CLAUDIA BLACK

In this chapter, you will learn about:

- The nature of the four Capacity for Trust Scales
- What you can do to develop your capacity for trust on
  each of the four scales

THE NATURE OF THE FOUR
CAPACITY FOR TRUST SCALES

Four attributes or criteria affect our capacity to trust a person or a situation: pragmatism, abstractness, complexity, and differentiation.[1] Each of these can best be understood as a continuum (see Figure 2).

We call these continua the Capacity for Trust Scales. These criteria are the components of our evaluating process as we decide whether to trust a person, group, or situation. We can look at these criteria separately but recognize that they are complexly interrelated. Changes on one scale often affect changes on one or more of the other scales. Where we are on each of the scales may shift over time. We will examine each of the four continua and how they relate to the development of our capacity to trust.

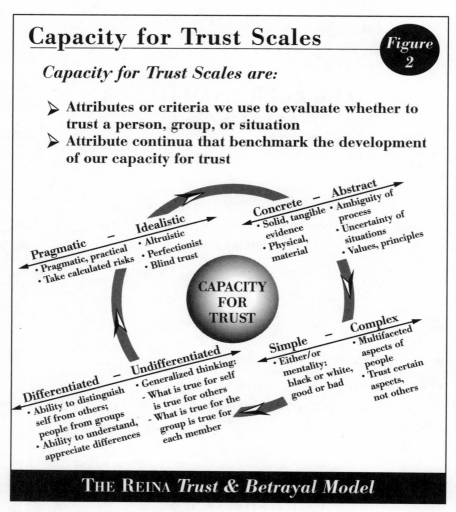

Figure 2   The Capacity for Trust Scales

Idealistic–Pragmatic

A person with an idealistic capacity for trust may have too much trust in self or others. A person who is pragmatic may take calculated risks and develop trust in incremental steps.

An idealistic person may blindly invest an unreasonable amount of trust in someone whom the person views as all-powerful. This was the case with the Jonestown cult members who followed their leader in committing mass suicide. Or an idealistic person may take unscrupulous risks with clients' money, as was the case with the Barings Bank securities trader in Singapore who brought that financial institution to the brink of ruin.

On the job, a person who is too idealistic may take unreasonable risks with a customer's project, believing it possible to overcome insurmountable challenges. Yet lacking the skills or resources to do so, the individual jeopardizes the company's reputation with that customer. Such a person takes unreasonable risks or makes unrealistic promises without knowing how to go about achieving the goals or keeping the promises. By contrast, a pragmatic individual would break the project down into manageable pieces and trust, realistically, that the goal can and will be achieved using the skills and resources available.

Another aspect of the idealistic capacity for trust at work is perfectionism. Perfectionists will trust no one but themselves to do the job because they are "the only ones who can do it right." If they delegate to others, they may have to accept a job not done to their own standards of perfection. People in the workplace today are forever pressed to do more with less. Individuals attempting to have every task done perfectly are idealistic and costly. On the other side of the scale, a person with a pragmatic capacity for trust does what is appropriate to get the job accomplished. Because pragmatists trust more in the abilities of others, they tend to collaborate more with others.

For certain jobs requiring an extreme amount of creativity, such as advertising, or for others requiring a willingness to take bold risks, such as trading on the stock market floor, the characteristics of an idealist are an asset. For other jobs, the attributes of a pragmatist are appropriate. But either taken to an extreme can be a liability.

Concrete–Abstract

An individual with a concrete capacity for trust needs solid, tangible evidence about self or others before being willing to trust. Such individuals tend to have a "prove it to me first!" attitude and a great need to feel that they are in control of themselves and the situation. For example, they tend to micromanage, becoming too involved in the details of projects. Unable to trust their employees to do the job, they fail to delegate, or when they do delegate, they continue to look over employees' shoulders,

PEANUTS reprinted by permission of United Feature Syndicate, Inc.

telling them how the job should be done. The *Peanuts* cartoon above illustrates an example of a concrete capacity for trust.

At the other end of the scale, people with an abstract capacity for trust are able to deal with the uncertainty of situations and the ambiguity of process. They are more comfortable letting go and trusting others to get the job done. For example, an individual with a concrete capacity to trust may need physical evidence before being willing to trust another. Someone with an abstract capacity for trust would be willing to trust a coworker's promise without tangible evidence.

It is crucial that senior leaders understand the organizational implications of the concrete–abstract scale. Many frontline employees operate at the concrete capacity for trust side of the scale (for example, hands-on production workers paid to produce concrete products). Many senior managers operate at the abstract capacity for trust side of the scale (for example, to create the vision and set the direction of the organization). One of the reasons for the breakdown in communication and growing distrust between senior management and frontline employees is that there is a "disconnect": they are each speaking a different language. Senior managers may "walk their talk" and live the corporate values (abstract criteria), but frontline employees want concrete evidence that they can trust senior management. "Show us the benefits package that was taken away!" "What happened to our 401(k) plan?" (concrete criteria). To begin to build trust with employees in low-trust situations, it is important that leaders think about what the other group's perspective is, use language the others can understand, and give them tangible evidence that the leaders keep their word and live by their principles.

Simple–Complex

An individual with a simple capacity for trust makes yes-or-no, black-or-white decisions about self or others, for example: "Joe is a total liar" or "Mary is always reliable." People with a simple capacity for trust are unable to see any shades of gray in another's personality. They may assail a person's (or their own) overall competence for making one mistake in a specific area. For example, after encountering some difficulty with data entry, an individual may exclaim in exasperation, "I can't do this project." People with a simple capacity for trust may be quick to give up on a project after encountering obstacles. They are their own worst critics, belittling themselves when things don't go as they had expected. They don't trust in themselves that they have what it takes to work through more complex problems.

By contrast, individuals with a complex capacity for trust are able to see the multiple sides of a person and the relative performance of each individual. They can appreciate that someone is reliable under certain circumstances but not others. For example, Steve, a manager who has a complex capacity for trust, knows that he can trust George, a very competent technician, to do an excellent job once he gets to work but can't trust him to be on time. He knows that Josette is good at solving computer problems but is not as strong interacting with customers.

Undifferentiated–Differentiated

There are two aspects to the differentiation scale. First, "How well do I differentiate others from myself? Do I assume that whatever is true for me is true for others?" Second, "How well do I differentiate others from various groups they might be a part of? Do I assume that whatever I perceive to be true for the group is also true for each of its members?"

Regarding the first aspect of this scale, a person who assumes that whatever is true for himself or herself is true for others is committing a form of indiscriminate projection. On the job, this can significantly hinder trust in a working relationship, especially if the person doing the projecting does not personally feel very trustworthy.

Regarding the second aspect of this scale, a person who assumes that what is true for the group is true for each of its members is guilty of a form of stereotyping. This leads to sweeping and inaccurate statements, such as "Management can't be trusted" or "The union has no clout."

These individuals make broad-based, blanket statements about individuals or groups without any basis for their validity or specific facts to back them up: "You can't count on anyone in that department" or "Those people are always trying to get something for nothing." Or they may take one small bit of truth about one individual and attribute it to everyone in the group.

Here is an example of an undifferentiated capacity for trust at work. Sam is a shop steward. Lowell, a new employee, looks very much like someone who betrayed Sam in the past. Consequently, Sam is reluctant to open up to Lowell and acts in distrusting ways toward him. Lowell reciprocates with similar behavior. As a result, the working relationship between the two is poor. What Sam doesn't realize is that his own projection onto Lowell, and Lowell's actions in response, created the very thing that Sam feared—distrust.

On the other side of the scale, persons who have a differentiated capacity for trust are able to discriminate individuals from groups and can understand and appreciate those individual differences. They are also able to make distinctions between groups (ethnic, religious, social, educational status, etc.) and do not make sweeping generalizations about groups.

As our capacity for trust develops and matures, we tend to rely on trust criteria that are more pragmatic, more abstract, more complex, and more differentiated than earlier in our lives.[2] That isn't to say that the more idealistic, concrete, simpler, and undifferentiated criteria are entirely abandoned. They may be used when appropriate in making decisions to trust ourselves or others. More concrete and simpler criteria may also be used when entering a working relationship where there is low trust. When there is low trust in a situation, it is important to make expectations concrete and communication simple and straightforward.

Our capacity to trust is not static but dynamic. It expands and contracts as it is updated by our positive and negative experiences. Everyone develops a unique trusting pattern or blueprint, reflective of one's experiences, which are unlike anyone else's. The positive and negative experiences we encounter, particularly during our developmental years, mold our capacity to trust and therefore our trusting patterns of behavior on the four Capacity for Trust Scales.

WHAT YOU CAN DO

Here we examine what individuals can do to increase their capacity for trust on each of the four scales. The information and exercises may be used for your individual development or for coaching others in developing their capacity for trust.

Idealistic–Pragmatic

As previously mentioned, people who are perfectionists and those who trust blindly demonstrate an idealistic capacity for trust. If these two types would like to explore other ways of relating to people, they may start the process by examining their core beliefs and begin the shift toward the pragmatic side of the scale.

Exercise 1: Examine your core beliefs. This exercise is about reframing or reprogramming your core beliefs about who you are and how you operate in the world. Your core thoughts and beliefs affect how you behave at work. Learning to trust involves going to our deep-rooted thoughts and feelings about ourselves. Many of these messages were planted early in our lives and are deeply embedded.

A number of perfectionist personalities are also Type A personalities who live intense, active lives with a high degree of stress. Giving yourself permission to relax, particularly in the midst of a hectic day, may not work for you, but find a time when you can be alone with your thoughts.

a. Spend quiet time with yourself at a convenient moment, perhaps at the beginning or end of your day. Give yourself fifteen to twenty uninterrupted minutes to reflect and quiet your mind.
b. Think about a core belief you may have about yourself: "Everything I do must be perfect" or "I'm not (big, smart, etc.) enough, so I've got to try extra hard" or "There's nothing I can't do: no job is too big."
c. Write down everything that comes to your mind about this core belief (including your emotions, childhood experiences, etc.).

d. Review what you wrote. Circle five to seven potent words from your notes, words or phrases that elicit a strong emotional response from you.
e. Think of one image or metaphor that sums up those five to seven words. (The image or metaphor represents your core beliefs.)
f. Flip the image over as you would a pancake. You are now looking at the opposite side. What new image is revealed?
g. Write five to seven words that describe this new image.
h. Next, write a whole new story or narrative based on these five to seven words. (They may include images, thoughts, ideas, or memories that support this new image.)
i. Put the new image on Post-it notes, and stick these in places where you will see them (on your desk, on your bulletin board, in your time planner, etc.). Make an affirmation—a positive statement in the present tense—using that image or metaphor.

Do this exercise several times. It provides an opportunity to replace self-limiting beliefs with more supportive ones. As we model new behaviors and set positive examples for others, we build more confidence and trust in ourselves.

This can also be challenging work. If some of the beliefs you hold about yourself seem to be obstacles that are too difficult to overcome, you might want to talk to someone, such as a professional counselor or therapist, about helping you change them.

Concrete–Abstract

Here we explore how you can help yourself or how you can help others become more trusting of themselves and others in ambiguous and uncertain circumstances. It may help you or them begin to let go of the need for control and shift toward the abstract side of the scale.

Exercise 2: Trust your intuition.   Another way to develop trust in yourself is to develop trust in your intuition. How many times have you ignored your intuition and were sorry you did? How many times have you followed what your head was telling you, yet you knew in your heart it was the wrong decision? Trusting our intuition requires us to trust ourselves.

The more you practice trusting your intuition and achieve positive results, the better you will get. Our intuition provides valuable clues into people's character and reliability. It is a like a barometer; it can sense concerns and incongruities in people's character. It is like sonar; it can sense the substance beneath people's words.

If we develop and use our intuition on a regular basis, it can be a reliable gauge of whether or not to trust someone. Trusting your intuition involves trusting more in yourself. The more you are able to trust in yourself, the more you are able to trust in people, and the more you are able to deal with the uncertainty of process.

a. Reflect on a time when you had a hunch about something and it came true. That was your intuition advising you.
b. Think about a decision that you need to make soon. Jot it down. Listen to your inner voice. What does your intuition tell you about the decision? What course of action emerges? Start with small decisions. Make a number of decisions following your hunches. Let this be an opportunity to begin practicing making decisions using your intuition.
c. After you have had some practice and success making decisions by trusting your intuition, graduate to more important ones. Record the results in a personal journal. Track your progress, and notice if there are any patterns or trends emerging.

Simple–Complex

To help begin the shift from a simple to a more complex capacity for trust, we need to allow ourselves to think out of the box.

Exercise 3: Think "out of the box." An individual with a simple capacity for trust does not trust himself to think creatively, "out of the box." Many of us grew up in the traditional educational system in this country. We were conditioned to think in terms of what was "correct" and acceptable in the eyes of the teacher. For some of us, our creative thinking was contained or squelched. Graduating to the organizational and professional worlds, we repeat this pattern by seeking the answers the boss is looking for rather than what we know and feel is the right answer. Unfortunately, what has been instilled in many of us is that the best ideas are in someone else's head. We fail to trust ourselves.

This exercise can assist in building our creative thinking skills and trusting our ability to think out of the box.

a. Think about a challenging problem you face at work. Record on a piece of paper as many ideas as come to mind that might resolve the problem.

b. Of the ideas that you generated, pick one or two that you think could solve the problem best. Trust your intuition in paring down the list. (Draw on Exercise 2.)

c. Reverse your perspective on how you are looking at the situation surrounding the problem on which you are working. If you are a manager, look at it from your employee's point of view. If you are an employee, look at it from your manager's point of view. What assumptions did you dislodge. and what new possibilities did you open up?

d. Consider the same problem. If you are a parent, what would your children have said about the problem when they were five years old? What would they point out as possible solutions? Children at this age tend to be more creative than adults because their creativity has not yet been conditioned out of them.

e. Concerning the possible solutions, what are the broader implications of your ideas? How do they fit into the bigger picture?

The process of contemplating and answering these questions will help you flex your creative and risk-taking muscles and teach you to trust yourself more by encouraging you to think out of the box.[3]

Undifferentiated–Differentiated

Shifting from an undifferentiated capacity for trust to a more differentiated one is a challenge. Most people's thoughts, feelings, and beliefs are deeply embedded and have been reinforced by family, friends, and coworkers over the years. Totally reversing these may be extremely difficult, but making some shift toward differentiation and expanding their capacity for trust is possible.

The following exercise may reveal more about yourself and help you shift toward greater differentiation.

Exercise 4: When in doubt, check it out.   Leaders cannot afford to make generalizations about anybody, particularly about people with whom they work. Question your assumptions and get the facts before making decisions.

Think about the kinds of sweeping generalizations you make about certain groups of people or situations. Then ask yourself honestly: every time you make such a generalization, don't you end up regretting it?

a. Think about an acquaintance at work with whom you have minimum contact but you were told by a coworker to be wary of.

b. The next time you interact with that person, step back from the interaction in your mind and simply notice: What is your attitude toward that individual? How are you coming across in interacting with this person? What sweeping generalizations are you making about the person?

c. Invest some time and get to know this individual better. Find out about the person's skills and strengths on the job, as well as personal interests and family, if applicable.

d. Now what is your attitude toward that individual? How are you coming across in interacting with this person?

e. Looking back at the sweeping generalizations you made earlier about this individual, how accurate were they? What did you learn about this individual and about yourself?

Developing our capacity for trust through self-awareness is a slow developmental process. It requires that we take the time to learn to listen to ourselves so that we can acknowledge our feelings, take responsibility for them, and trust ourselves.

IDEAS IN ACTION

Here we examine what leaders can do to expand their capacity for trust. The questions may also be used by a leader or a facilitator to coach other individuals or a team.

Questions to Consider

Reflect on the following questions, and record your thoughts.

1. Draw a continuum labeled "idealistic" at one end and "pragmatic" at the other. Mark an X on the continuum at the point where you might fall. Remember, being pragmatic is associated with being practical

and willing to take calculated risks. Being idealistic is more perfec-
tionistic or, conversely, tending to trust blindly and excessively.
Drawing on material from this chapter, how do you see your position
on this continuum affecting how you trust yourself and others?
Thinking about this scale, what might you do differently in the
future to improve your capacity to trust?

2. Draw a continuum labeled "concrete" at one end and "abstract" at
the other. Mark an X on the continuum at the point where you might
fall. Remember, being concrete is associated with needing solid, tangible evidence. Being abstract is associated with feeling comfortable
with uncertainty and ambiguity.
Drawing on material from this chapter, how do you see your position
on this continuum affecting how you trust yourself and others?
Thinking about this scale, what might you do differently in the
future to improve your capacity to trust?

3. Draw a continuum labeled "simple" at one end and "complex" at the
other. Mark an X on the continuum at the point where you might
fall. Remember, being simple is associated with experiencing things
as either-or, black or white, good or bad. Being complex is associated
with experiencing more shades of gray, seeing people and situations
as multifaceted.
Drawing on material from this chapter, how do you see your position
on this continuum affecting how you trust yourself and others?
Thinking about this scale, what might you do differently in the
future to improve your capacity to trust?

4. Draw a continuum labeled "undifferentiated" at one end and "differentiated" at the other. Mark an X on the continuum at the point
where you might fall. Remember, being undifferentiated is associated with generalized thinking, seeing yourself and others as very
much the same, and making broad generalizations. Being differentiated is associated with identifying and valuing individual differences.
Drawing on material from this chapter, how do you see your position
on this continuum affecting how you trust yourself and others?
Thinking about this scale, what might you do differently in the
future to improve your capacity to trust?

4

UNDERSTANDING BETRAYAL

The greater the loyalty and involvement,
the greater the betrayal.
JAMES HILLMAN

In this chapter, you will learn about:

- A definition of betrayal
- The nature of betrayal
- The high cost of betrayal in the workplace
- The effect of betrayal on our capacity for trust
- Major and minor betrayals
- How we betray ourselves and others

A DEFINITION OF BETRAYAL

Betrayal means different things to different people. In this book, *betrayal* refers to an intentional or unintentional breach of trust or the perception of such a breach. Intentional betrayal is a self-serving action done with the purpose of hurting, damaging, or harming another person. Unintentional betrayal is the by-product of a self-serving action that results in people being hurt, damaged, or harmed.

    Betrayal occurs on a continuum from major intentional betrayal to unintentional minor betrayal (see Figure 3). Major intentional betrayals

Betrayal

Figure
3

Betrayal is:

➤ **A breach of trust or the perception of such a breach**
  • **On a continuum from major to minor**
  • **Committed intentionally or unintentionally**

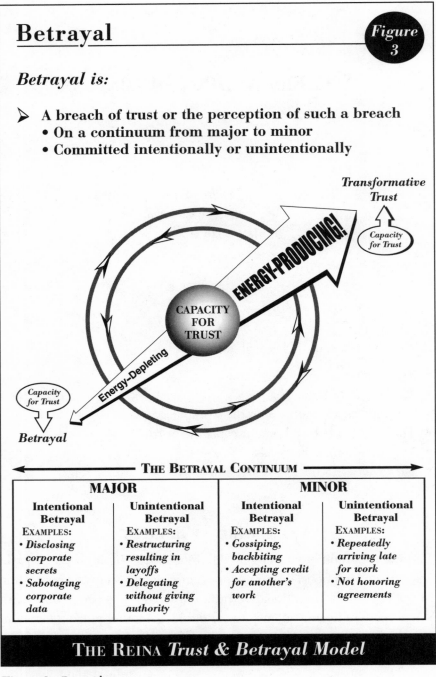

THE REINA *Trust & Betrayal Model*

THE BETRAYAL CONTINUUM			
MAJOR		**MINOR**	
Intentional Betrayal	**Unintentional Betrayal**	**Intentional Betrayal**	**Unintentional Betrayal**
EXAMPLES: • *Disclosing corporate secrets* • *Sabotaging corporate data*	EXAMPLES: • *Restructuring resulting in layoffs* • *Delegating without giving authority*	EXAMPLES: • *Gossiping, backbiting* • *Accepting credit for another's work*	EXAMPLES: • *Repeatedly arriving late for work* • *Not honoring agreements*

Figure 3   Betrayal

are carried out to hurt and harm. Unintentional minor betrayals are incidental to other actions.

Major betrayals are often the by-products of fear and avarice. They are caused by people not honoring their commitments or deceiving fellow coworkers to further their own ends. As one concerned employee said, "It is especially painful when we are stabbed in the back by those closest to us without warning. It knocks you off your feet."

Most betrayals are minor. These are the more prevalent acts that alienate employees from their managers, their peers, and their subordinates. These subtle betrayals seem innocent and unimportant yet can grow to more severe hurts and contribute to much of the negative feeling that employees have toward their bosses, each other, and their companies. Not keeping one's promises, gossiping, and hoarding pertinent information are everyday occurrences of minor betrayal. However, *minor betrayals can escalate into major betrayals if not addressed and resolved.* This occurs when minor betrayals stay alive in people's minds. Over the course of time, they become bigger than the actual event. The cumulative weight of their own thought processes makes them major.

The placement of an experience along the *betrayal continuum* depends on the perception of the betrayer's intent and the impact on the receiver—in other words, the degree to which a receiver perceives that the individual intended to cause hurt, damage, or pain to the receiver and the degree of hurt, damage, and pain actually caused or inflicted. For instance, accepting credit for someone else's work may be a minor intentional betrayal in one circumstance, but if one person gains greatly at another's expense (for example, if someone gets promoted as a reward for something that in reality a coworker deserved credit for), it becomes a major intentional betrayal.

THE NATURE OF BETRAYAL

The opportunity for betrayal in any relationship at work or in our personal lives depends on the degree of trust we have of that individual, situation, or organization. People often wonder if their expectations will be met. If an individual has few or no expectations and trust is low, the chances of

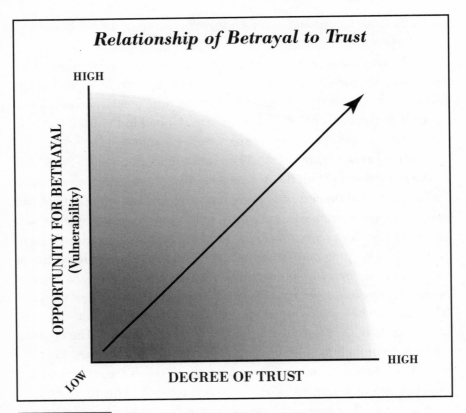

Relationship of Betrayal to Trust

SOURCE: Developed in collaboration with Richard Weaver, Ph.D.

being betrayed are not great. Consequently, that individual is not particularly susceptible to disappointment, hurt, or betrayal. However, if one has high expectations, be they warranted or not, one is more vulnerable to betrayal. The illustration above reflects the correlation between degree of trust and opportunity for betrayal.

THE HIGH COST OF BETRAYAL IN THE WORKPLACE

Organizations depend on trust to function. We must trust that Department A will produce work of sufficiently high quality, coworkers will complete their assignments properly and on time, bosses will treat people fairly, and company executives will make decisions to keep the company healthy. When we trust in that way, we can focus on doing our jobs and contributing to both ourselves and our organization. Betrayal destroys the fabric of the relationships that keep our organizations operating. Major betrayals demolish the essential trust that has existed, while minor betrayals eat away at it bit by bit.

Major betrayals are traumatic experiences that diminish people's energy, cloud their thinking, sap their motivation, and derail their productivity. Rather than focusing on doing their normal jobs, betrayed individuals attend to protecting themselves and possibly taking revenge on whoever betrayed them. Their productivity plummets.

To move employees out of betrayal toward trust, it is important first to understand the nature of betrayal. In an effort to rebuild trust, leaders need to understand what betrayal is, the relationship of betrayal to trust, and the effect major and minor betrayals have on our capacity for trust in ourselves and others.

THE EFFECT OF BETRAYAL ON OUR CAPACITY FOR TRUST

Whether a betrayal is major or minor, the experience affects our capacity for trusting ourselves and others. People's emotions vary in intensity of pain, depending on their perceptions of the severity of the betrayal. Leaders are in denial if they don't believe that people have feelings about business transactions. Betrayal goes to the core of human vulnerability; it cuts through us to our deepest emotional layers. For example, one vice president of an international telecommunications company reflected on being betrayed by his boss: "I had to get out. I got myself transferred as soon as possible. I couldn't work for someone I didn't trust." Betrayal is a deeply felt issue—so much so that people use physical words to describe their emotional states. As another manager in a pharmaceutical company said, "I really got beat up in that board meeting this morning."

MAJOR BETRAYAL: TRUSTING OTHERS

A major betrayal can decrease our capacity for trusting others. As stated, major intentional betrayals are deliberately planned to manipulate others for self-gain. The perpetrators know that their actions will hurt others, and they justify them with self-serving arguments. Our level of trust in these individuals decreases dramatically, and our capacity to trust others can plummet as well.

Brenda, a designer for a major advertising agency in New York, was severely shaken when a trusted friend and coworker stole her ideas for an ad campaign she had been working on. Brenda was further incensed when her colleague received a large year-end bonus as a reward for her deceitful actions. From that point on, Brenda cut all personal ties with this individual and became extremely cautious about sharing her ideas with anyone.

Our level of trust and vulnerability determines the depth of betrayal we feel. In Brenda's case, she trusted her colleague very much—perhaps unwisely and unrealistically. As a result, she was quite vulnerable and caught off guard.

Though unintentional betrayal is a by-product of a self-serving action, it can have hurtful consequences. Losing a job or being demoted may be the by-product of downsizing or restructuring, but people end up hurt nonetheless. Once an organization starts downsizing, the consequences are never-ending. Like betrayal, the negative consequences and the negative energy are larger than the act itself. The betrayal is implosive; it sucks productive energy from employees—especially those worrying about whether they are going to have a job next month. Betrayal is systemic; it affects the whole system. For example, downsizing affects the morale of the whole company, not just the people losing their jobs. It shuts down the whole system, removes trust, destroys relationships. As one frustrated employee said, "I can do five hundred things to build trust in a relationship; then I do one act, and all the trust is gone in a split second."

Every day on the job, leaders betray employees unintentionally. If you give an employee the responsibility but not the authority, trust, and support needed to do a project, you have destroyed the full potential of that employee's contribution to the company.

A major betrayal, intentional or not, is shocking and devastating. It grabs us when we least expect it. What we thought was dependable is not dependable; what we thought was permanent is not permanent. Our world is turned upside down, and we are tossed into emotional chaos. We wonder, "Where can I place my trust now?" "Whom can I trust?"

MAJOR BETRAYAL: TRUSTING OURSELVES

A major betrayal can decrease our capacity to trust ourselves. Because it slams us over the head and pierces us at our core, it is a profound experience. Betrayal is so profound because it shakes our confidence and causes us to doubt ourselves. It wounds a relationship at a deep level. Betrayal is usually taken personally, and it is rarely forgotten.

When we are betrayed, our emotions are raw; we feel vulnerable and wounded to our core. Major betrayal evokes our deepest feelings because it touches the very center of our vulnerability. As one shaken coworker said, "You make yourself vulnerable to the other person, and he uses your own sword to betray you." Being rejected against our will can severely damage our self-esteem, leaving us feeling powerless. Losing a job or being passed up for a promotion can bring up feelings of worthlessness and may be devastating to our capacity to trust. As one distraught employee explained, "My experience of betrayal is that I am standing on a rug and the rug is suddenly pulled out from under me. I am tumbling helplessly out of control."

Through self-exploration and self-awareness, we are able to shift out of the negative feelings of betrayal and view them as a stepping-stone to personal and spiritual growth. However, most of the time, rather than working constructively with our pain, the more typical reaction is to give ourselves over to anger and resentment. In fact, the words *betrayal* and *traitor* come from the same Latin root, *tradere,* meaning "to hand over, deliver, place in the hands of." When we "hand ourselves over" to the anger, pain, and grief of betrayal, we betray ourselves. Our emotional responses and actions perpetuate the pain.[1] When we act as victims after being betrayed, we lose the opportunity to learn and grow from the experience. If we take the traditional response to betrayal and operate out of fear, control, and manipulation, we end up sabotaging ourselves, as well as others.

In *Journey from Betrayal to Trust,* Beth Hedva, drawing on the work of James Hillman, defines the following five emotional ordeals of betrayal, if one chooses a traditional response to the betrayal.[2]

1. Righteous resentment, which leads to obsession about the betrayer. "How could they do this to me? It's not fair! I've given seventeen of the best years of my life to this company. I don't deserve to be treated like this!" This fuels the desire for vengeance and vindication.

2. Bitter resignation springing from denial of the positive and seeing only the negative in one's betrayer. "I always knew they were only concerned about making money and didn't give a damn about their employees. I should have expected this."

3. Attributing your betrayer's negative traits to all others deemed like your betrayer. "That's just like big business" or "You know how that company is." Generalization fuels cynicism, prejudice, and bigotry.

4. The abandonment of your ideals, essential values, or vital dreams. "At my age, I'll never get a job like I had with Company X, again. Why bother! Companies today aren't interested in experienced workers—they just want to use you and then throw you away and hire some kid to take your place." Denial of one's essential self as expressed through denial of one's personal values and visions leads to self-betrayal.

5. Denial of your existential right to be, to live your dreams. This leads to fear, control, and manipulation—making rules to protect against future betrayals. "I may get another job, but I am never going to give my heart and soul to my work again. I'll do just enough to get by—nothing more, nothing less."

A personal crisis can teach us a lot about ourselves. Whether betrayal occurs in our private lives or our work lives, it can be an opportunity for inner growth, if we are willing to work through the feelings and endure the pain. In the next chapter, we will explore steps individuals can take to help heal themselves; in Chapter 10, we will explore the steps leaders can take to help others heal from betrayal.

MINOR BETRAYAL: TRUSTING OTHERS

One minor betrayal will probably not decrease our capacity to trust others. However, as minor betrayals accumulate, they will eventually affect individuals' capacity for trust toward one another and create distrust between them. Distrust is defined as the "feeling that another's intentions and motives are not sincere; that they have ulterior motives."[3] The *cycle of distrust* shown in the illustration below depicts how distrust begets distrust and grows toward betrayal.

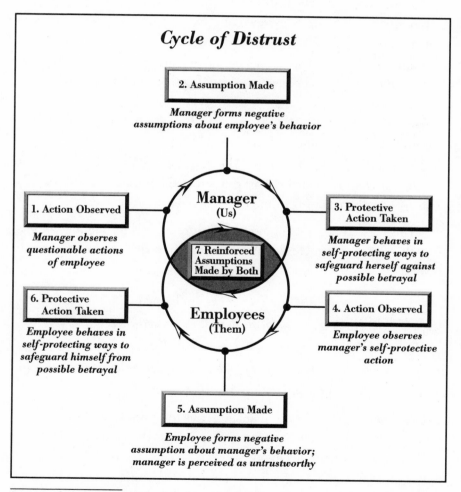

Cycle of Distrust

2. Assumption Made

Manager forms negative assumptions about employee's behavior

1. Action Observed

Manager observes questionable actions of employee

Manager
(Us)

7. Reinforced Assumptions Made by Both

3. Protective Action Taken

Manager behaves in self-protecting ways to safeguard herself against possible betrayal

6. Protective Action Taken

Employee behaves in self-protecting ways to safeguard himself from possible betrayal

Employees
(Them)

4. Action Observed

Employee observes manager's self-protective action

5. Assumption Made

Employee forms negative assumption about manager's behavior; manager is perceived as untrustworthy

SOURCE: Adapted with permission from the works of Kathleen Ryan, Steve Simon, and Rosa Carrillo

The cycle of distrust can start anywhere. It is a combination of negative assumptions and self-protective behavior in a self-reinforcing pattern that repeatedly traps both managers and employees:

1. *Action observed:* A manager observes a questionable action by an employee.
2. *Assumption made:* The manager forms a negative assumption about the employee's behavior and the employee.
3. *Protective action taken:* The manager behaves in self-protecting ways to safeguard herself from possible betrayal.
4. *Action observed:* The employee observes the manager's self-protective action.
5. *Assumption made:* The employee forms a negative assumption about the manager's behavior, concluding that the manager is untrustworthy.
6. *Protective action taken:* The employee behaves in self-protecting ways to safeguard himself from possible betrayal.
7. *Reinforced assumptions made:* The manager believes the employee's behavior is untrustworthy. This reinforces the negative assumptions she originally made regarding the employee.

This cycle repeats itself in many different ways throughout all levels of the organization. Here is an example of how this cycle may play out at work.

Sue, a recently hired manager, is charged with the task of developing the fabrication unit into a self-directed work team. She has been informed by her boss that this is a challenging group and that the group members may try to "push the boundaries" to see what they can get away with to test their new boss.

1. *Action observed:* Sue, the manager, calls ten-minute stand-up meetings with the team each morning. She notices that one employee, Tom, is late three times in one week.
2. *Assumption made:* Without checking out her assumptions with the specific employee, Sue forms an opinion that the employee is trying to test the company's policies regarding tardiness.

3. *Protective action taken:* At the next meeting, Sue makes a statement that she will not tolerate any abuse of the tardiness policy.

4. *Action observed:* Tom is astonished at Sue's comments regarding tardiness. He feels that he has been openly reprimanded in front of his coworkers and feels humiliated and offended.

5. *Assumption made:* Tom concludes that the boss is insecure and is very controlling, making a big issue of the tardiness. He also decides that the boss is insensitive: "She didn't even ask me why I was late."

6. *Protective action taken:* Tom challenges Sue, demanding to know the number of minutes one is allowed before being deemed tardy.

7. *Reinforced assumptions made:* Sue witnesses the employee's aggressive and defensive behavior. The fact that he even asked the question illustrates this employee's lack of accountability. This reinforces the negative assumptions Sue originally made regarding Tom.

Distrust breeds distrust and ultimately betrayal. When a leader comes from a place of fear and caution, worrying about whether she can trust an employee, her behavior can backfire and cause the very distrust and betrayal she seeks to avoid.

Most betrayals are not intentionally malicious and are not designed to hurt others. They are the product of overworked, stressed-out employees trying to do more with less. Yet these minor betrayals can create significant hurts, which lead to major betrayals. And major betrayals result when people realize the extent to which they have been quietly misled. The discovery of deception, dishonesty, or indirectness may prompt an abrupt exit from an effective working relationship between individuals. When people are allowed to get away with breaching trust in minor ways, it becomes easier to betray in major ways. The cumulative effect of these minor betrayals eats away at trust and damages working relationships between individuals and the organization.

How We Betray Ourselves and Others

Individuals will overlook the negative ways they affect people to the extent that they lack self-awareness and are controlled by their own pressing needs. We may be contributing to the betrayals that happen to others in ways we may not be aware of. The following questions illuminate how our capacity for trust influences the degree to which we betray ourselves and others.

Do We Expect to Be Rejected?

If we expect to be rejected or criticized, we might constantly test people's loyalty and commitment to us: "You'll have to prove to me that you're trustworthy first." Being constantly on the defensive, we are ready to run from or "beat up on" those individuals who may present a danger to our delicate sense of safety and identity. People who have a low capacity for trust in themselves may project their inability to trust in others. People who need solid or tangible evidence in order to trust their coworkers exhibit a concrete capacity to trust.

Do We Contribute to Conflict?

Expectations of conflict generate the very conflict we fear. Our attitude influences our interactions with others. Do we enter a potential disagreement on the defensive? As one factory worker said to a coworker, "If you are looking for a fight, by golly, I am going to help you find one!"

Thought is creative. If we expect trouble, our defensive actions may contribute to the very thing we fear. People who have a low capacity for trust in others may exhibit protective behaviors that cause other individuals to react in a similar fashion. We have seen in the *cycle of distrust* that demonstrating distrust begets more distrust.

Are We Mostly Preoccupied with Our Own Problems?

If we are constantly preoccupied with our own problems, we may be totally unaware of the impact of our behavior and actions on others. If we are fostering an attitude that the world is treating us poorly, we rarely feel responsible for the pain we cause others. People with a low capacity to trust in themselves may feel victimized by their circumstances. They may come across as needy and are emotionally draining on their coworkers. Their preoccupation with themselves causes them to be unaware of their actions. These people break promises, miss deadlines, and are insensitive to the problems they cause others.

Do We Create Enemies Unnecessarily?

If we are preoccupied with a frantic search for certainty and predictability, it may prevent us from understanding the complexity of dynamic relationships at work. For example, in conversations with coworkers, these individuals may have little tolerance or patience for differences with others. They may come across as self-righteous, speaking in absolutes and thinking in simplistic, black-or-white, good-or-bad terms. People who don't understand or disagree with the points they are hearing may react with a verbal attack. For these people, life is a battle to be won, and the goal is being right and winning at all costs.

People with this approach have a simple capacity to trust and may have a limited ability to deal with the uncertainty of new situations. For example, when facilitating a team meeting, they may come across as domineering: "My way is the right way." They may have difficulty leading a dialogue session that lacks a formal structure.

Do We Discount People?

If we feel hurt, embarrassed, or frightened in our association with someone, we may conjure up an elaborate mental smoke screen to protect ourselves from feeling the memories of past painful experiences. By degrading and dehumanizing the other individual, we disengage ourselves from any awareness of their worth and well-being.[5] History has shown that major wars have been fought by countries that could not resolve their conflicts peacefully. They have discounted other nations or ethnic groups by labeling them the enemy and portraying them in nonhuman, demeaning terms. It is easier to drop a bomb on our enemies if we convince ourselves that they are evil.

In the workplace, people fostering this perspective have an undifferentiated capacity for trust. They are unable to identify individuals from the groups in which they are members and may prejudge others without fully understanding them. Because these people have a low capacity to trust others, they don't cooperate with others. As a result, information and resources to accomplish the job are not readily shared, working relationships suffer, and the organization is cheated out of their potential performance.

As we have seen, betrayal happens every day. It happens in major events and in minor oversights. It is done intentionally and unintentionally. People betray us; we betray them; we even betray ourselves. Betrayal destroys trust between individuals, among teams, and throughout organizations. Knowing how to deal with it is essential. Dealing with betrayal is the topic of the next chapter.

IDEAS IN ACTION

Here we examine what leaders can do to understand betrayal. The questions and exercise may also be used by a leader or a facilitator to coach other individuals or a team.

Questions to Consider

Reflect privately on the following questions, and record your thoughts. If you are working with a team, have team members share their thoughts. Discuss how attitude toward trust affects how people in your team or organization relate to one another and how work gets done.

1. Describe a major personal or work-related betrayal that you have experienced. Remember, a betrayal is an intentional or unintentional breach of trust or the perception of such a breach. How did you feel emotionally when it happened to you? What did you think about the situation? How did you respond to this betrayal?

2. Describe a minor unintentional and a minor intentional personal or work-related betrayal that you have experienced. In what ways did your experience of them differ? What were the feelings you had in response to each of these examples?

3. Describe a major unintentional and a major intentional personal or work-related betrayal. How did it feel when these happened? Was there a difference in the ways you experienced them because one was intentional and one was not? How were these feelings similar and different from the minor betrayals? How did you respond to each of these betrayals?

Application Exercise

Refer to your responses to Questions 1–3 regarding major and minor betrayals. Categorize your experiences using the betrayal continuum below as a template.

$\longleftarrow$ ─── **BETRAYAL CONTINUUM** ─── $\longrightarrow$

MAJOR		MINOR	
Intentional Betrayal	**Unintentional Betrayal**	**Intentional Betrayal**	**Unintentional Betrayal**
EXPERIENCES:	EXPERIENCES:	EXPERIENCES:	EXPERIENCES:

DEALING WITH BETRAYAL

Life's most liberating discoveries are often reserved for
times when we feel most wounded or broken.
JOHN AMODEO

In this chapter, you will learn about:

- How we deal with betrayal
- The Seven Steps for Healing from Betrayal
- What we can do to heal from betrayal

Chest aching, stomach churning, she splashed water on her
face as she fought back tears of shock, horror, and deep hurt.
Judith could not believe what she had just heard. She honestly thought
she and Mike were totally aligned. What a way to find out they were not!

Judith had been given the responsibility of overseeing the design
and development of a major building complex by the company presi-
dent. She asked Mike to work with her on developing the proposal out-
lining the approach to the project. She had tremendous respect for
Mike's skill and talent, and they had worked well together in the past.

Judith felt that she and Mike developed a solid proposal and
looked forward to reviewing it with the president. At the start of the
review meeting, she could not believe her ears when the president

*mentioned that Mike had stopped into his office that morning—behind
Judith's back—and had announced that he had major concerns about
the proposal and about Judith's ability to oversee the project. Judith was
flabbergasted.*

HOW WE DEAL WITH BETRAYAL

As with Judith, betrayal catches most of us off guard. Major betrayals
often seem to come out of the blue. To cope and get through the initial
shock of our experience, we may be inclined to repress our pain and let
ourselves get swept up in confusion. Many of us become quite skillful at
distracting ourselves by keeping busy and substituting work and materi-
alistic concerns in an attempt to shield ourselves from feeling our pain.
Others will seek outside entertainment or turn to drugs, alcohol, or food
to assuage their pain. Either way, "through our denial we betray ourselves
by being unconscious to our underlying need, which is to understand and
heal, so that we may return to a state of 'wholeness.'"[1]

In organizations, we see people at all levels feeling betrayed. We see
leaders feeling betrayed by inconsistencies in the systems of which they
are a part. We see people feeling betrayed as a result of the way decisions
have been made or changes orchestrated. Often betrayal is not a result of
what happened but rather *how* it happened. Leaders may honestly
believe that the decision to downsize, to merge, to cancel a product line,
to restructure a department, or to bypass someone for promotion was
absolutely in the best interest of the long-term health of the organization.
However, they cannot and must not ignore the impact of those decisions,
particularly the impact of the manner in which those decisions were carried out. The real betrayal occurs when decisions that affect peoples' lives
are carried out without awareness and sensitivity to their impact.

In such cases, a double betrayal occurs: the leader's own self-
betrayal in failing to honor the integrity and spirit of leadership and a
betrayal of the people and organization the leader leads and serves. Both
result in loss.

Few of us know how to deal with the emotional pain of betrayal
because our culture doesn't encourage reflection and genuine expression

of our feelings. Experiencing a major betrayal is like experiencing a death. We have feelings of loss—of plans, of jobs, of dreams, of relationships, of trust in others or ourselves. Our hearts ache, our capacity to trust may be bruised, and our innocence is tarnished.

Trust is not necessarily the same as naiveté, but before a betrayal, we may be oblivious to the risks involved in trusting. James Hillman offers an interesting perspective of betrayal that allows us to see the larger purpose it may serve. According to Hillman, trust cannot be fully realized without betrayal. Only after we have experienced betrayal, when we fully know the risks and can trust anyway, is true trust established.[2] Honoring the trust in our relationships is like taking care of the health of our body. Many people assert that we can't really appreciate our health unless we have been seriously ill. That same line of reasoning suggests that we can't really know and appreciate trust until we have experienced betrayal.

This does not mean that we should run back and restore our trust in our betrayers or in the psychological shields we throw up to protect ourselves against future betrayals. On the contrary, before we approach anyone else, we need first to allow ourselves to take in our experience, honor it, and work with it. We need to allow ourselves to go through our own process of healing. Since major betrayals are like a death and we experience a loss, we need to go through a grieving process. When we do so, we open the door to healing. We are then available to assist others with their healing.

Whether we are betrayed or betrayer, the experience of betrayal provides an opportunity to discover more about ourselves. This is something many of us want. We want to understand. We want to arrive at meaning that enriches us. But we often ask ourselves how: How do we deal with the depth of pain we are feeling? How do we resolve past hurts so that we see hope in rebuilding relationships?

As noted, experiencing a betrayal has much in common with experiencing a death. There is a sense of loss. Healing after a betrayal, as after a death, requires some form of grieving. In her examination of death and dying, Elisabeth Kübler-Ross defined the steps of the grieving process: shock, anger, denial, rationalization, depression, and acceptance.[3] Our Seven Steps for Healing from Betrayal (see Figure 4) build on her work

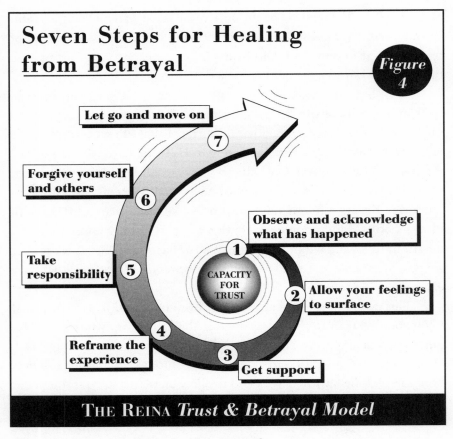

Figure 4 — Seven Steps for Healing from Betrayal

and provide manageable steps to help us move through our hurt and depression to acceptance and wholeness.

Like health, healing is a function of participation. Although the steps are numbered sequentially, working through them is not necessarily linear. The steps represent phases of the healing process. Different people go through the phases in different ways. You may progress through them one at a time, or you may be in multiple phases at the same time. Or you may have completed one step and moved on to the next only to reexperience aspects of the earlier step again. Feelings come in waves; there are highs and lows, ebbs and flows.

The Seven Steps for Healing from Betrayal are intended to serve as a framework for individuals and leaders as they work through the painful feelings of betrayal. The Ideas in Action section at the end of this chapter explores how leaders may use the Seven Steps to assist teams. In Chapter 10, we explore how the Seven Steps may be used to help organizations heal from betrayal. The Seven Steps address healing on the individual, team, and organization levels because healing needs to occur at all levels. For teams and organizations to heal from betrayal, individuals need to heal first.

THE SEVEN STEPS FOR HEALING FROM BETRAYAL

Step 1: Observe and Acknowledge What Has Happened

Moving from betrayal to trust starts with self-discovery. The first step in moving out of betrayal is awareness. Notice what you are experiencing, and acknowledge what is so. Observe your thoughts: "I was taken advantage of," "He double-crossed me," "I gave my best to this company and this is what I get?" As a result of these observations, acknowledge your true feelings: "I'm angry," "I'm depressed," "I feel taken advantage of," "I feel betrayed," "I feel like hell!" Do not try to analyze, understand, or intellectualize your thoughts and feelings; just "simply notice" them.[4] We must consciously observe and acknowledge our thoughts and feelings before we can do something about them.

Step 2. Allow Your Feelings to Surface

Give yourself permission to feel. Once you are consciously aware of your feelings, allow yourself to feel your pain—all of it. You have experienced a loss; acknowledge and grieve for that loss. We need to honor and respect our emotions. They are central to the healing process. They are real and have a right to be expressed. The most effective way out of the pain is *through* the pain. Use your body as an instrument of healing by allowing yourself to feel your emotions. If you feel anger, feel angry. If you are afraid, feel afraid. It's OK to feel lousy.

Recognize that nobody else can do it. This is a job nobody can do for you. In our professional lives, there are many tasks we can delegate to people, but grieving is not one of them. This is your work. We may attempt to avoid grief, but the only effective way to experience true healing is to work through it. For those willing to embrace the grieving process, there is light at the end of the tunnel. Healing does provide deeper value and meaning to the pain you are experiencing, though that may be hard to believe while you are in it.

Give yourself quiet time alone. Each of us needs to create time and space in our lives to get in touch with and explore our feelings. For some people, reflective time spent writing in a journal may be therapeutic; others may prefer physical exercise such as walking, running, or working out at the gym. What is important is not what you do but how you do it. Choose an activity that helps you get in touch with your painful feelings rather than escape and avoid them.

Say no to guilt. The betrayal may occur only once, but we relive it in our minds a thousand times. If you are like many people who are hard on themselves, you may become obsessed with guilt and worry. You replay over and over again the injustices that you suffered. By doing so, you hurt yourself even more. Although it is important to feel our feelings in order to grieve, feeling guilt and worry are of no positive value and are not helpful emotions for healing. They drain your energy, cloud your thinking, and clutter your emotions.

Step 3: Get Support

Healing from major betrayal is like any major change process: it is difficult to do alone. We all need support. Yet it may be difficult for us to reach out. When we have been deeply hurt, we are feeling vulnerable, and our instincts may be to draw back. We may find ourselves less trusting of others. As a result, we may not feel inclined to share our experience.

Although this reluctance is completely understandable, you must force yourself to reach out. This is a time to be good to yourself, and getting support is one way of doing that. It may be helpful to consider the options available to you and select the one with which you are the most comfortable. You may turn to a colleague, a friend, or family member. Alternatively, you may turn to a member of the clergy, a counselor, a support group, or a professional coach.

Have these people share the feelings you are presently experiencing or assist you in reconnecting with painful feelings of your past related to your present circumstance. Use this support to help you confront feelings of helplessness, hopelessness, and powerlessness so that you may reestablish your self-esteem and return to a fuller sense of self.

Step 4: Reframe the Experience

Put the experience into a larger context. The healing process is an inquiry. The questions you ask yourself will guide your journey. Reflecting on the questions you ask will provide you with understanding, awareness, and truth.[5] Typical questions you may find yourself asking include the following:

- Why did this happen?
- What is the purpose of this event in my life at this point?
- What messages do I need to hear?
- What lessons do I need to learn?

Reflecting on these questions will help you sort out your thoughts and emotions and arrive at greater insight. Listen to your inner voice; it will provide the answers to these questions. The answers will allow you to gain clarity regarding your feelings, think about things in a different way, and reframe what you are experiencing.

Look for the greater purpose. Reframing our perspective on a betrayal can help us see that there is a greater purpose to this experience. Through reframing, we are able to convert our experience of betrayal from a trauma to a "rite of passage" in life. We are able to use the hurt and pain as stepping-stones to spiritual growth and an opportunity to develop our capacity for trust in ourselves even further. Reframing the betrayal experience may help us realize that there is an inner resource, a higher power within, that brings us through every experience in life, including betrayal, and that there is value in what we have experienced, painful as it was.[6] We see the benefit to our personal development. Whether the betrayal was intentional or unintentional, we learn, by consciously working through the Seven Steps, to listen to and trust in our higher self. We see life's process as one that helps us renew, heal, and transform our experiences. We deepen our capacity to trust ourselves. We deepen our understanding and respect for relationships.

Step 5: Take Responsibility

Take responsibility for your role in the process. After feeling betrayed, many people are obsessed with blaming the culprit and getting revenge. There is no benefit to this perspective. Rather than dwell on who is at fault, we must take responsibility for our reactions. We have a choice in how we will respond to our experiences. It is far more productive to accept responsibility for working things through than to place blame and cast judgment. Healing and growth require us to be accountable for our behavior and the choices we made that may have contributed to the betrayal.

In any relationship between two people, both contribute to the unfolding dynamics. When we accept responsibility for our reactions and resulting choices, we are in a better position to examine what led up to the precipitating event and how we may have contributed to it. We may ask ourselves:

- What role did I play in the process?
- Am I disowning the problem?
- Am I making excuses or diverting blame away from myself?
- What could I have done differently?

We all have choices in any situation.

Step 6: Forgive Yourself and Others

Forgiveness is a gift we give ourselves. People may perceive the concept of forgiveness differently. One view is that forgiveness is a gift we give ourselves to free ourselves from the burden of bitterness and resentment. In this light, forgiveness is more for us than for the other person. When we forgive, *we* are the ones who benefit first. Forgiveness provides us with an opportunity to heal our wounds more rapidly. If we wait for the person who betrayed us to apologize, we make ourselves hostages of the very person who wronged us in the first place.[7]

Forgiveness is healing. Holding on to negative feelings of anger, resentment, and bitterness can deplete our spirit and interfere with our capacity to trust. However, with forgiveness, we not only help heal ourselves but also create an opportunity for healing to happen between us and the person who hurt us.

Forgive others. In the process of forgiving, we experience hurt, hate, healing, and coming together.[8] In our hating, we cannot forget how much we hurt. With a major betrayal, we may want our betrayer to hurt as much as we do. With a minor betrayal, we may not have the energy to wish the betrayer well. Though none of us wants to admit it, when we hate, it is extremely difficult to heal. To shift from hate to healing, personal insight is critical. Literally, we need to shift our focus from our betrayer to our wounded selves. We need to detach from the person who hurt us and let go.

Forgiveness may be likened to a kind of "spiritual surgery," a cutting away of the wrongs our betrayer did to us and a separating of the person from the deed. When we can do this, we are able to see our betrayers as people with needs and feelings.[9] And when it comes right down to it, we are mirrors of each other. At the bottom of it all, we are like them and they are like us.

Final healing occurs when we invite the person back into our lives. This is challenging because it depends as much on the other person as on us. Both parties have to be willing to come together. If the other person is not, we must heal within ourselves.

To have reconciliation between the two parties, we expect our betrayers to listen and hear our claims, acknowledge and honestly apologize for what they did, understand the depth of the pain they caused us and feel the hurt we felt, and make new promises that they intend to keep. They must give back more than what was taken.

How do we know forgiveness has begun? When we can think about individuals who betrayed us and are willing to wish them well. In situations when people are unwilling and unable to come together, we can still forgive them and free ourselves—in our minds and in our hearts.

Forgive ourselves. Most of the betrayals that occur at work are unintentional. Hurting others does not mean we are bad people. Most of the time we hurt others by oversights, rushing, cramming to do more with less time, energy, and money. However, the more decent and self-aware we are, the more we feel the pain we caused others.

Forgiving ourselves is as important as forgiving others. In forgiving ourselves, we need to be candid, clear, courageous, and concrete. First, we need to be candid by honestly facing the facts, admitting our wrongdoing and our faults, and acknowledging the pain we caused. Second, we need to be mentally clear and put our inner critic on mute. We need to clear our heads to make way for an open, forgiving heart. We need to forgive ourselves for the wrongdoing we did. Third, we need to be courageous and face ourselves and others we have wronged and let go of any shame. Finally, we need to be specific about what precisely we are forgiving ourselves for.

Step 7: Let Go and Move On

Reflect on the experience. In looking back over the experience, what have you learned about yourself and others that you can use in the future? What will you do differently next time? How will you approach future relationships?

Choose to act differently. Like learning a new skill, learning to relate to yourself or others in a different way takes practice and time. Start with small steps. Experiment with what works and what doesn't. Focus on what is in your power to control. Trust in yourself and in the process.

Focus on being. We spend much of our professional lives focusing on where we would like to go in our careers and what we need to do to get there. We spend little or no time reflecting on who we are and what kind of person we are in our relationships. Many leaders neglect this area. If we want to develop as leaders of people, we need to know ourselves. We change by not trying to be something other than who we are but by being fully aware of who we are and honoring that knowledge.

Lighten up. Be careful not to take yourself too seriously. You should of course be conscientious about your work and your job, but taking yourself too seriously puts distance between you and others. Cut yourself and others some slack!

There is no spontaneous healing when it comes to going through the pains of betrayal and rebuilding trust in ourselves and our coworkers. In fact, it takes a lot of hard work. However, working through these Seven Steps will help us heal, let go, and move on. Each of us will do it in our own way. We will need to spend more time on some steps than on others, especially when working through our feelings. Since intense feelings come in waves, we may progress through several steps, only to go back and deal with additional feelings that may surface. We may also be in multiple steps at once. The sequence through the process is not important. What is important is that we, in our own way, go through the process with honesty and integrity. By facing betrayal in a conscious way, we can move toward greater understanding of the value of the experience and develop a greater capacity for trust in ourselves and in others. Only in this way can we find value and meaning in the pain and form enriched relationships in the future.

IDEAS IN ACTION

Here we examine what leaders can do to deal with betrayal at work. The questions and exercise may be used by a facilitator to coach other individuals or a team.

Questions to Consider

Reflect on the following questions, and record your thoughts.

1. Consider the Seven Steps for Healing from Betrayal. Were you able to complete all seven steps when you were betrayed? If yes, what were your feelings as you completed each step? How did it feel when you were able to move on?
2. If you were not able to complete all seven steps, where did you stop? What contributed to your halting at that point? Were you frustrated at not completing the steps? What ideas did you gain from this chapter that will help you complete the steps?
3. In the future, how are you going to use the Seven Steps for Healing from Betrayal? How do you see their use reducing the total pain felt by you and others?

Application Exercise

The following questions are intended to facilitate dialogue and begin the healing process as a team. The nature of this process requires that the Seven Steps be facilitated by skilled facilitators. It is essential that they ensure the psychological and physical safety of the group to enable the healing process to begin. Implement confidentiality agreements or ground rules with the group before beginning the process.

1. *Observe and acknowledge what has happened.* How can we start the healing process? Reflect on the circumstances that caused you or your teammates to feel betrayed. You may use the betrayal continuum at the end of Chapter 4 to list and categorize betrayals within your group or team. Share those findings with your teammates.

2. *Allow your feelings to surface.* What feelings are present regarding each of these betrayals? Notice how you feel when you are betrayed. List the emotions you feel. Do you feel angry? Vindictive? Hurt? Sad? In pain? Acknowledge your feelings. When you share your experience with others, remember to use "I" statements rather than blaming others: "I feel angry" rather than "You made me feel angry." This is easier said than done. When we are in pain, we want to strike back and get revenge on the person who caused that pain.

   Notice how your teammates feel about being betrayed. Listen to understand what your teammates are saying. It is helpful not to get defensive or make excuses for what happened. Simply acknowledge what they are saying. People need to know that they are heard for the healing process to begin.

3. *Get support.* What kind of support, if any, do we need? After allowing feelings to surface, notice if you feel rejected or abandoned. The betrayal experience may trigger a fear of loss, separation, or abandonment from our past as well as the present (loss of security, status, or a paycheck). What support do you need to help you deal with these feelings? Individually, you may want or need to talk to someone you trust about your feelings. You may seek professional assistance (human resource professional, employee assistance program counselor, psychotherapist, etc.). As a team, it is important to have a skilled facilitator assist group members in dealing with their feelings.

4. *Reframe the experience.* How can we reframe the experience? Look at the big picture. What were the surrounding or extenuating circumstances that led to the betrayal? Which circumstances were beyond your control? Which were within your control?

5. *Take responsibility.* What do we need to do to take responsibility? What part did you play in the process? What did you do or not do that contributed to the betrayal? Is it possible that you did not express yourself clearly or set firm boundaries with the other person? Do you have a need to make the other person wrong so you can be right? How did you betray yourself or the other person in the relationship? What actions can we take to take charge of the situation?

6. *Forgive yourself and others.* How can we forgive ourselves and others? Are we ready to forgive? What needs to happen for forgiveness to take place? Realize that each of us has positive and negative sides, strengths and weaknesses. Notice the worst negative trait of your betrayer, and ask yourself if you ever acted or felt that way.[10] We betray ourselves when we try to negate the fact that we have a shadow side and attempt to disown the part of ourselves that we find distasteful. Acknowledging your weaknesses helps you forgive and have compassion for yourself and others.

7. *Let go and move on.* What do we need to do to let go of these feelings and perceptions? What needs to be said or done to put this experience behind us? Have each team member reflect on these questions and share his or her needs with the group. Define and record action steps and implementation strategies to bring closure to this process.

TRANSACTIONAL TRUST

There are the three types of Transactional Trust:

Contractual Trust, Communication Trust, and

Competence Trust. Each has specific behaviors that

build trust and maintain relationships in the workplace.

Transactional trust is created incrementally

and is reciprocal. In other words,

you've got to give trust to get it.

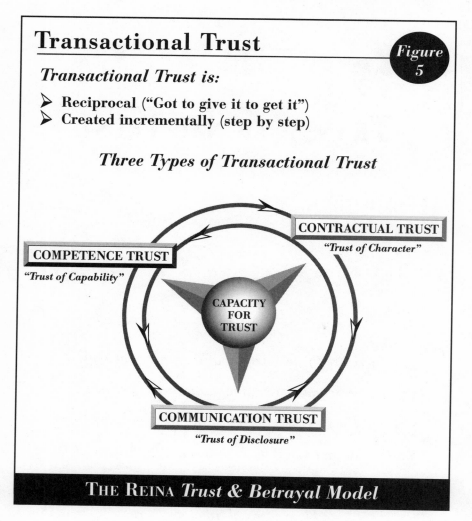

Transactional Trust

Figure 5

Transactional Trust is:

➤ Reciprocal ("Got to give it to get it")
➤ Created incrementally (step by step)

Three Types of Transactional Trust

CONTRACTUAL TRUST
"Trust of Character"

COMPETENCE TRUST
"Trust of Capability"

CAPACITY FOR TRUST

COMMUNICATION TRUST
"Trust of Disclosure"

THE REINA *Trust & Betrayal Model*

6

CONTRACTUAL TRUST

*Trust is the expectancy held by an individual or a group
that the word, promise, verbal or written statement of
another individual or group can be relied on.*
JULIAN ROTTER

In this chapter, you will learn about:

- A definition of Contractual Trust
- The nature of Contractual Trust
- Behaviors that foster Contractual Trust

A DEFINITION OF CONTRACTUAL TRUST

Contractual trust is managing expectations, establishing boundaries, delegating appropriately, encouraging mutually serving intentions, keeping agreements, and being congruent in our behavior. How we practice these behaviors demonstrates the quality of our character as perceived by ourselves and others. Therefore, we call contractual trust the "trust of character" (see Figure 5A).

THE NATURE OF CONTRACTUAL TRUST

Contractual trust implies that there is an understanding in the relationship that we will do what we said we would do. It may be delivering a product, providing a service, sharing information, attending a meeting,

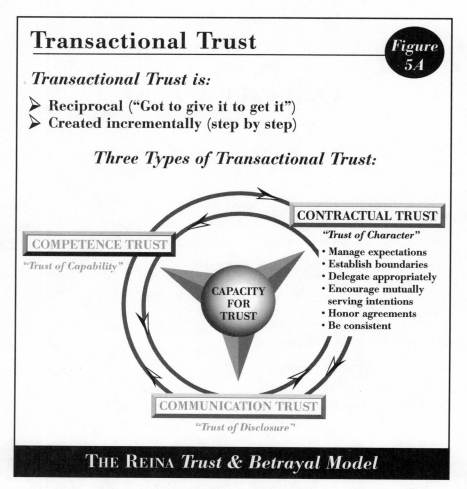

Figure 5A The Contractual Form of Transactional Trust

producing a report, or simply returning a phone call when we promised. Contractual trust deals with keeping agreements, honoring intentions, and behaving consistently. Confidence in the intentions, consistency, and reliability of individuals to honor their commitments makes or breaks contractual trust on the job.[1]

Contractual trust forms the basis of most interactions in the workplace. Employees have a strong need to have confidence in the intentions, consistency, and reliability of their leaders. Likewise, leaders have a need to have confidence in the intentions, consistency, and reliability of their people to meet business objectives. The greater a leader's span of responsibility in the organization, the more the leader must rely on others to meet the objectives and the more imperative it is that the leader effectively model the behaviors that foster contractual trust.

But what does contractual trust mean in everyday terms? Honor your word? Keep your commitments? You can tell when someone gives you a halfhearted commitment. How does it feel on the receiving end? Weak? Flaccid? Like a limp handshake? We are not inclined to put much credence in that kind of commitment. It leaves us with a hollow, empty feeling inside.

Contractual trust in a relationship provides clarity surrounding what we can honestly and truly expect from people and what they can honestly and truly expect from us. It brings clarity to what we can count on and what they can count on. Knowing the answers to these questions provides a foundation on which trust may grow. Keeping our word to ourselves and others is powerful! When we keep our commitments, we build contractual trust.

Committed action, not empty words, builds contractual trust in relationships, between individuals, on teams and in organizations. For example, the new vice president of operations of a large manufacturing plant in the Northeast was getting oriented to his job. He met Larry, manager of the shipping department, and asked him, "So Larry, how many people work for you?" Larry replied, "About half of them!" Larry himself was new, with the company only six months, and had not yet earned the respect and commitment of his people. Earning their trust is critical to earning their commitment.

BEHAVIORS THAT FOSTER CONTRACTUAL TRUST

Specific actions in six different areas are crucial to building contractual trust. Let us look at each in turn.

Manage Expectations

Managing expectations is essential to contractual trust: our expectations of others, their expectations of us, and our expectations of ourselves. "Expectations are like self-fulfilling prophecies. What we expect of people is often what we get."[2]

Thus a leader's expectations of people greatly influences their performance. Unfortunately, many leaders expect poor performance and get it. But leaders can empower people by setting high expectations and trusting in people's competence. If more is expected of employees and they are given the support they need to work toward those expectations, they will be motivated to meet and even exceed the original expectations. And by setting expectations high, a leader demonstrates trust in people's abilities. It is in essence saying, "I trust you to do this work."

Employees' expectations of leaders also affect contractual trust. People would like leaders to consider their expectations when making decisions. Expectations reflect needs. At times, expectations are not met because they have not been identified or understood. A lack of clarity regarding expectations causes misperceptions and misconstrued intentions. When people's expectations are not met, they may feel a range of emotions. They may feel disappointed, discounted, taken advantage of, angry, and hurt. The result may be distrust and feelings of betrayal. As a food service production supervisor expressed it, "I bent over backward for you, I've done so much for you—and you do this to me? Never again! And just wait until next time, when you really need something!"

When people respond to disappointment or betrayal in this manner, they may act like victims; they may become passive-aggressive and feel the desire to get even. "I'll show you," they say under their breath. This revenge gets played out on the job in a variety of ways. People may choose to withhold information or not share it fully with others; they may not work with the same vigor or commitment to meet deadlines; at the extreme, they may sabotage the efforts of others.

There are two kinds of expectations when dealing with others: explicit and implicit. Both kinds have their place, are appropriate and useful in the everyday workplace, and contribute to the development of contractual trust.

Explicit expectations.   Explicit expectations are clearly stated and understood requirements. Trust comes out of a clear understanding of responsibility; that is, what is expected of an individual and what the individual may expect in return. When people have a clear understanding of what is expected of them and they meet those expectations, trust grows. When expectations are not clear and go unfulfilled, trust erodes.

Charlie needs to be direct. He is too vague in his directions and in his requests of his technicians. So when his employees don't deliver what he expected of them, he gets frustrated and blows up at them. His behavior further pushes his employees away and weakens the fragile trust that may exist between them.

Healthy working relationships require clear expectations, whether it involves starting a project, forming a task force, developing a unit, or working on any number of initiatives. When people don't find out what is expected of them until they run into a wall, cross a boundary, or fail to get a promotion or pay raise, it is too late. In this situation, people may experience a range of emotions from disappointment to betrayal. Clarity around expectations affects relationships and productivity, determining what can get accomplished. Performance is significantly enhanced when leaders are clear regarding the expectations they have of employees and convey them candidly and explicitly. Employees want to know what is expected of them and "need to understand, up front, the rules for engagement," a telecommunications company division manager pointed out.

Janet, a new supervisor, was hired for her high level of technical skills. Yet her first year's performance on the job was miserable. Ralph, Janet's manager, took her aside and began coaching her. He set out clear expectations conveying his trust in her basic abilities. Janet needed help understanding what her customers, her employees, and the company valued and the things she needed to do to produce that value. During the next eighteen months, Ralph worked with Janet, giving her frequent coaching and feedback. Janet was able to turn around. She focused on the things that added value. In fact, she won three awards within a year and a half, which made her even more valuable to the company.

Seeing that Ralph believed in her, Janet was able to believe in herself. Her capacity for trust in herself, Ralph, and the company grew deeper over time.

Contractual trust between managers and employees serves as a foundation of understanding on which boundaries may expand and contract. People are given more freedom to do their jobs and are able to manage that freedom appropriately. Obviously, the flip side of that coin is responsibility. As employees are given more freedom, leaders expect them to take on commensurate responsibility. Likewise, trust erodes when employees are given a task or a project but not given the corresponding authority to carry out the assignment. When employees are given the necessary resources and authority to fulfill expectations, they get the message that they are trusted.

Implicit expectations. Implicit expectations are unwritten, unspoken requirements, agreements, or understandings between people.[3] Cultural norms of the organization influence implicit expectations: "That's the way we do things around here." Previous experiences also contribute to implicit expectations: "The person who held that position before always did it this way."

Unfortunately, implicit expectations are often difficult to notice until we feel the consequences of not having met them. For example, if a new hire takes liberties that he was accustomed to at his old job without checking to see if they are appropriate in his new work environment, he may be setting himself up for a downfall. Furthermore, the more responsibility one holds in an organization, the greater the implicit expectations are.

Managing relationships up, down, and across the organization are important to the success of any leader. When expectations are worked out specifically and in detail, contractual trust begins to develop. However, during times of change, expectations become increasingly difficult to manage. They can become vague, and the level of contractual trust may begin to decline. Relationships may be jeopardized when expectations are not clear. To help gain clarity around expectations, leaders will benefit by reflecting on the implicit contracts they have with the people with whom they work. Leaders may consider the degree to which the contracts are understood and mutually beneficial. They may need to clarify implicit expectations and make them explicit.

By and large, people want to meet the expectations others have of them or would like the opportunity to negotiate if they feel the expectations are unreasonable. People want to be successful and want the organization they work for to thrive. People seek work environments where expectations are understood. People look to leaders and expect leaders to take the time to build relationships and create environments where expectations are shared, discussed, and understood.

Establish Boundaries

Establishing and maintaining clear boundaries is another behavior that fosters contractual trust. Boundaries assist in defining the roles of individuals and the purpose of a multitude of organizational structures, such as teams and departments. As such, they play a strong role in developing contractual trust. Boundaries help define the relationship between individuals, teams, units, and the organization. Although some theorists contend that boundaries separate people, boundaries may actually aid in connecting people by serving as points of exchange.[4] In these points of exchange, relationships are built and trust is further developed. In addition to creating a strong sense of solidity and identity, boundaries provide a sense of safety within a system that is necessary when building trust.

Delegate Appropriately

Delegation provides another opportunity for developing contractual trust. When delegating, leaders invest trust in their employees to do their jobs. Delegation demonstrates trust in people's abilities. It further defines people's roles and the boundaries of their responsibilities. To develop contractual trust in delegating, individual objectives need to be clear, explicit, visible, and mutually understood. This awareness helps employees develop their capacity for trust in themselves and the organizations in which they serve.

Because trust is a reciprocal process, it is critical, "when delegating projects, to create a two-way feedback loop with employees to ensure mutual understanding," one project account manager explained. When people operate under an assumption of shared understanding rather than an explicit understanding, they set themselves up for some form of betrayal. Although it may be an unintentional, minor betrayal, it is a betrayal nevertheless. Disappointment and frustration often result, and the level of trust diminishes. "When you delegate a project to employees without giving them the authority, feedback mechanisms or support to do the job well, you set yourself and the employees up for failure, and you put your company at risk," said the senior partner in an international accounting firm. Contractual trust decreases when people fail to receive what they expect or what they need to accomplish what they have been asked to accomplish.

Agreements work both ways. When your people deliver, you deliver! When delegating, you need to be consistent in your requirements regarding quality of work and your expectations. Trust is created through consistency of behavior. Consistency creates boundaries within which work relationships may perform.

Diane, a project manager in an engineering firm, was overseeing a major project in which Mark played a role. The project was promised on time and on budget to the client. Diane reviewed the parameters three times with Mark and was confident that they were understood. However, Mark's part of the project came in over budget and behind schedule. In Diane's questioning of Mark regarding his performance, Mark's response was, "Other things came up." Diane was furious with Mark and felt betrayed. She had given her word to the client, and now her word meant nothing.

Diane, however, did not abandon the relationship. "I gave him another chance. I had a heart-to-heart talk with him. I reviewed the expectations, clarified his questions. I checked for his understanding by having him repeat back his understanding of the expectations. Then I asked for his agreement to the new expectations. In validating the agreement, I put the burden of responsibility on him."

Diane continued to clarify expectations and manage Mark's performance every time she gave Mark a project. Over the next six months, Diane's consistent and firm behavior with Mark began to pay off. Within a year, Mark was one of the most reliable project engineers in the group.

Encourage Mutually Serving Intentions

Mutually serving intentions exist when individuals support each other in striving for success. When two individuals make an agreement to deliver a product, information, or services to each other, there is a mutual expectation they each will deliver on time and they will work toward meeting each other's goals. When people support each other's intentions, contractual trust is reinforced and our trust in others is enhanced.

Trust is facilitated when people are interested in each other's welfare. It is necessary that both parties give something to the relationship before trust can be established. Building trust is reciprocal. Yet many people are "unable to see this and are unwilling to risk being the first one to trust for fear of exposing themselves and then being vulnerable to the other party."[5] Our perceptions of another's intentions influence our tendency to trust or be suspicious. What we perceive or attribute to another's intentions will affect our relationship with them. An attorney admitted, "I perceive that Jeff tries to manipulate me for his own advantage. As a result, I don't deal with him unless I have to!"

Unfortunately, if trust is low in a situation, most people tend to choose only one motivation out of numerous possibilities. They tend to personalize intentions by casting themselves as the intended recipients of the other person's harmful actions. Such people are responding with a narrow perception and a low capacity for trust.

If we read more into other people's motivations than is actually there, we end up more suspicious and less trusting of them. Conversely, if we read too little into their intentions, we may be overly trusting and end up being duped. One hotel administrative supervisor said, "I thought my officemate was completely honest in her dealings with me; I didn't realize she was talking behind my back."

To build trust, we have first to be true and honest with ourselves. There are times when our behavior produces results we did not intend. For instance, we may have inadvertently left someone out of a decision-making loop, we may not have included all pertinent parties in the circulation of a report, or we may have left someone off the invitation list to an off-site planning meeting. Such actions, though not intentional, cause others to feel hurt, disappointed, and perhaps angry.

Although the outcome is not what we initially intended, we still need to assume responsibility for what occurred. People are especially frustrated and disappointed when leaders, in particular, refuse to accept responsibility for "unintentional" acts. Hearing "but that was not my intention" strikes them as a lame defense. They consider that response an abdication or shirking of responsibility or a diversion of blame. People understand that the outcome may not have been intentional; nevertheless, they still look to their leaders to be responsible.

Denying responsibility or blaming others or the surrounding circumstances may allow one to save face in light of an awkward situation, but only temporarily. It certainly does not build trust and is often experienced as a betrayal. Contractually, employees look to their leaders to talk straight with them and to admit and accept their role in performance outcomes. Every employee really deserves nothing less.

Honor Agreements

Honoring agreements speaks to individuals' dependability in carrying out their commitments.[6] When we keep agreements with ourselves, we feel good, we know we can be counted on, we feel trustworthy. When we keep agreements with others, we empower the relationship; we build and nurture the trust between us. "If I repeatedly meet my agreements, I enhance the capacity for trust between us," said a financial analyst. "There is an emotional payback you get from keeping your word and following through on your agreements—you feel better."

When we break agreements with ourselves—for example, if we fail to meet deadlines, even if they were a bit unrealistic—we disempower ourselves. We lose trust in ourselves. If we repeatedly fail to meet our agreements, we decrease our capacity to trust ourselves and our sense of trustworthiness.

When we break agreements with others, we disempower the relationship and compromise the trust between us. If we repeatedly fail to honor our agreements, we decrease the capacity for trust in our relationships. The comments of a frustrated telecommunications manager reprimanding her employee, illustrates this point: "Rose, if you can't do it, tell me. If you say you are going to come through and don't deliver, I am not able to meet my commitments. You lose credibility with me, and I lose credibility with my customers."

However, by renegotiating broken agreements, we can renew and possibly strengthen the relationship. "This is a real opportunity to make or break your credibility," an international consultant pointed out. When rebuilding trust that has been broken, expect backsliding. This is not easy work and requires a great deal of commitment. Yet as leaders, we need to persist in our commitments, regardless of the pitfalls. Know that you will make mistakes and employees will say, "I told you so." This comes with the territory of leadership.

Trust becomes more solidified when our actions match our words and we follow through on our intentions. Words help articulate our expectations, but actions demonstrate our trustworthiness. "The most difficult challenge for a leader is to behave consistently, on a day-to-day basis, in a way that reflects the organization's vision and values."[7] Walking the talk, as important as it is, is not as easy as it sounds.

So we must be careful of what we promise. Leaders get into trouble when they want to make a good impression and promise the world, only to fall drastically short on their promises, lose credibility, and damage their reputations. If we fail to keep our promises, it is harder for us to regain our trust. Unfortunately, people will forget the promises you kept and remember the promises you didn't keep.

For leaders, an information systems manager pointed out, "trust is earned, not by our words, but by our actions." And "trust declines when we fail to act consistently or fail to follow through on our commitments."[8] Through their actions, leaders demonstrate their commitment and belief in people and the organization. By fulfilling their responsibilities and commitments and delivering what they promised, leaders produce business results and build their employee's trust.

Be Consistent

Consistency in the behavior of leaders, when predictable, creates boundaries for employees. It gives them parameters within which they can operate. Further, it helps them remain connected to leaders when all else is changing. Likewise, when leaders are not consistent or congruent or true to their word, it is abundantly clear to employees. "How can I trust him when I don't know what he is going to do?" they ask. "He is like a loose cannon. He shoots from the hip. I never know what he is going to say." Inconsistent behavior makes it hard for people to know what they can expect or where to place their trust.

We need to make a distinction between actions and behavior. Consistency in actions is a challenge for leaders of organizations in an ever-changing global marketplace. In fact, it may be detrimental at times. The direction you set for your company eighteen months ago may no longer be appropriate because of evolving market conditions. By contrast, consistency of behavior, based on principles and values, is a necessity, especially in the rapidly changing business environment. There is no easy answer to this dilemma. Inconsistency in behavior may be perceived as dishonest or self-serving (or both) and will undermine trust. This is especially true when the people observing changes don't understand the rationale behind the shifts in direction.[9]

George is a "techie" who has accepted a human resources position. He wants to do a good job, but his perception of what the job entails and his natural behavioral style are totally at odds. He must act in a way that does not come naturally or easily to him. In interacting with people, he is always in great conflict between how he believes he should act and his natural behavioral style.

His boss, the company CEO, has a set of expectations for George in the performance of his job, but these have never been clearly articulated. In addition, George does not get sufficient feedback on his performance and as a result is struggling in the position. The gap widens as unspoken expectations increase. The CEO is communicating his dissatisfaction nonverbally.

At this point, there is a breakdown in trust on both sides. The CEO doesn't perceive that he can depend on George to do what is expected of him. George can't trust the CEO to give him the clarity and coaching to inform him of what is expected of him.

Using his natural behavioral style, George has the foundation or platform to do an excellent job. But George is in the wrong job. (Incongruent behavior is typical of a poor job fit.) As a result, George is not performing his job responsibilities well, and trust between him, his boss, and his constituents is deteriorating.

Leaders need to work hard at being consistent for themselves and for others. Consistency is a form of being true to oneself. Because people's perceptions become their reality, when there are gaps between what a leader does and what he or she is perceived to be doing, distrust with employees is created. One senior manager of a utilities plant put it bluntly: "More trust is lost or gained by whether a leader is true to his word."

We may not notice how important consistency, and the resulting trust, is when times are good and things are going well, but it is absolutely vital when times are bad and things aren't going so well. Trust among employees and leaders is what will get an organization through the tough times.

In developing contractual trust with employees, it is important that the appropriate parties acknowledge that they have entered into a contract. An expectation has been set. Some leaders establish written contracts with their employees, often in the form of a written summary. These are not used as weapons to hold over someone's head. On the contrary, they are used to develop trust—to make implicit expectations explicit and to establish clear boundaries. They are further used as a vehicle to track progress and to identify areas where additional support and resources may be needed. They provide a foundation for success.

Once the contract is established, whether it is in writing or verbally understood, it must be managed for trust to prevail. Both parties have a responsibility to themselves and others to honor agreements, monitor activities, measure performance, continually review commitments, and renegotiate when necessary. Relationship is work. Developing trust takes time, energy, and attention.

IDEAS IN ACTION

Here we present questions and exercises that leaders can consider in building and maintaining contractual trust with their people. The questions may also be used by a leader or facilitator to open communication between individuals on a team.

Questions to Consider

Reflect on the following questions, and record your thoughts.

1. Where in your personal and work life do you experience high levels of contractual trust?

2. What examples can you cite of you or others using the management of expectations as a means of fostering contractual trust? How have

your efforts to deal more effectively with expectations contributed to higher levels of contractual trust?

3. In what ways have you already used the establishment and maintenance of boundaries as a productive way to protect and improve contractual trust? How can you use this approach even more in the future?

4. How have you used delegation in ways that have fostered contractual trust? Do you create clear agreements when you delegate? If so, how do you do this? If not, how might you improve your delegation skills?

5. Are you conscientious in honoring your agreements? After reading this chapter, what actions might you take to improve your track record on commitments even further?

6. When you take action, do you consider the interests of others as well as your own self-interest? Do you look to see if your actions will hurt someone else? How do you check on that?

Application Exercises

A. The following questions are intended to facilitate dialogue as a team. Reflect privately on the behaviors that create contractual trust. Share those thoughts with your teammates. Discuss and list what needs to happen with each behavior.

1. *Manage expectations.* Are there expectations I have of my employees, peers, or boss that are not clear and explicit? If so, what implicit (unwritten, unspoken) expectations or working contracts should be explicit?

2. *Establish boundaries.* Are there boundaries that need to be established with my employees, peers, or boss? Are we aligned on goals, roles, and procedures? What is each person's level of commitment to the goals, roles, and procedures?

3. *Delegate appropriately.* When delegating a project or a job to an employee or peer, do I make sure the objectives are clearly understood with tangible, measurable results of performance by specified due dates?

4. *Encourage mutually serving intentions.* Are my intentions self-serving or mutually serving when interacting with my employees, peers, or boss? In my interactions, do I operate with hidden agendas? What interactions do I need to clear up with others?

5. *Honor agreements.* Do I honor my agreements? If I am unable to keep an agreement, do I renegotiate with the affected individuals promptly? What agreements do I need to renegotiate?

6. *Be consistent.* Am I generally consistent in my behavior in relating to others? Are my actions congruent with my words? Do I "walk my talk"? In what actions am I not congruent with my words? In my interactions with others, do I operate with integrity?

B. Reflecting on the six behaviors that foster contractual trust, where are we as a team, on the Contractual Trust Matrix below? Place an X in the most appropriate box.

Contractual Trust Matrix					
BEHAVIORS	**FREQUENCY OF OCCURRENCE**				
	Never	**Occasionally**	**Halftime**	**Usually**	**Always**
Manage expectations					
Establish boundaries					
Delegate appropriately					
Honor agreements					
Be consistent					
Operate with mutually serving intentions					

7

COMMUNICATION TRUST

Truth is the property of no individual but the treasure of all.
A. P. STANLEY

In this chapter, you will learn about:

- A definition of Communication Trust
- The nature of Communication Trust
- Behaviors that foster Communication Trust
- How Communication Trust builds relationships

A DEFINITION OF COMMUNICATION TRUST

Communication trust is the willingness to share information, tell the truth, admit mistakes, maintain confidentiality, give and receive constructive feedback, and speak with good purpose. How we practice these behaviors demonstrates our willingness to disclose and the quality of that disclosure. Therefore, we can characterize communication trust as "trust of disclosure" (see Figure 5B).

THE NATURE OF COMMUNICATION TRUST

Trust influences communication, and communication influences trust. The two are very closely related. When leaders readily and consistently share information and involve employees in the running of the business,

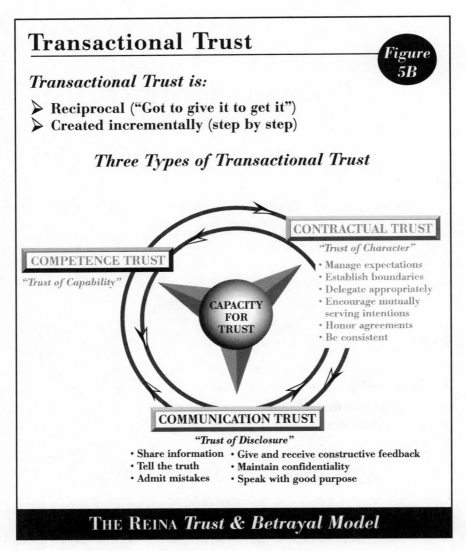

Figure 5B   The Communication Form of Transactional Trust

it not only affects the trust between them but also affects productivity and profitability. People have to know what is happening if they are to work efficiently and effectively and be enthusiastic about what they are doing. Experience shows that high levels of trust can be established if managers let employees know what is influencing the business.[1] We encourage leaders to follow a general rule: "If I am not sure whether I should or should not communicate, I should."

BEHAVIORS THAT FOSTER COMMUNICATION TRUST

There are a number of behaviors leaders may practice that contribute to building and maintaining communication trust at work. Working through the lens of our model, we explore several of those behaviors.

Share Information

Do we provide information willingly to others? Or do we simply "tell them only what they need to know"? This is an important question to ask ourselves, and answering it requires a high degree of honesty with ourselves. Some leaders assume that in the position they hold, they are obligated only to tell employees what they specifically need to do their job. This couldn't be further from the truth. Limiting the information shared sends a message to employees that they are not trusted to manage information, that they do not deserve to have information. It is not in the best interest of the organization for leaders to be secretive.[2] When employees don't have all the information or the correct information, they assume the worst, especially in the midst of a change effort. This causes misunderstandings, needless concern, and distrust. When people don't have the facts, they tend to make them up, and rarely are they positive. This is where gossiping and the grapevine get activated, deflecting time and energy away from day-to-day responsibilities.

The president of a large manufacturing operation asked us to assist him in assessing the climate of his organization following a significant change process. The changes the organization made were not producing the desired results. The president had a sense that there was some "disconnect" in the level of understanding among the employees regarding the change. He sensed that employees were not aware of the conditions that precipitated the need for change and the ways in which the change was designed to benefit the entire organization. Although the president felt the detachment, he could not quite put his finger on it and was unsure of how to address it.

As we engaged with the organization and worked with people in all types of positions, we were able to confirm that a disconnect did exist. When provided with a safe forum to share their perspectives, employees shared their experiences regarding how the recent changes had been managed:

> There was lack of communication and much miscommunication regarding changes that were taking place. People felt lied to. Human Resources had to pick up the pieces after being left out of the decisions. Even if management didn't have the answers, they simply needed to say they don't know. It appeared as though leadership was operating in a chaos mode. To effectively steer this ship in the direction [in which] we need to head, the top management team needs to present a united front.
>
> Every level of management has paid a great deal of lip service to the working troops. The information flow has dried up. Instead, we must rely on the rumor mill or grapevine for information. We never really know how accurate it is. We feel as though we have been cut adrift and are floating aimlessly.

The president's instincts were right: the disconnect existed between senior leadership and the employees at large. People mentioned that the lack of open information sharing contributed to employees' losing confidence and trust in leadership and the future direction of the company. As a result, employees were no longer able to trust what they heard and certainly were not able to contribute fully to the organization.

When information is not shared or there is a perception that information is not shared, employees feel betrayed. They feel as though they have not been trusted, and therefore trust in leadership erodes. A government employee said, "I guess management doesn't trust that we can handle the information. So we are left in the dark."

The typical leader knows the importance of giving employees the information they need to do their jobs. Leaders are aware that they have an obligation to help employees accomplish what they are expected to accomplish.[3] Given this knowledge, one cannot help but wonder, "Why is information withheld?"

There are numerous reasons why leaders do not readily share information. Some are conscious and deliberate, while others are not. For example, some information may be sensitive or confidential and therefore inappropriate to share. In these circumstances, it is helpful to indicate to people that you are not at liberty to disclose all information. People are able to understand and respect the need for confidentiality and leadership's responsibility to maintain it. When a leader says, "I am not able to share all the pertinent information at this time," that degree of honesty actually enhances people's trust in their leader. Interestingly enough, even though they are not provided with "all the information," they feel informed.

It is also true that there are individuals who consciously choose not to share information for a variety of reasons, the most common of which is fear of loss of control. They fear that not being the only ones "in the know" will reduce their value or power in the organization. This is most true in periods of major change, when people are feeling particularly vulnerable and perhaps threatened. They respond out of a need to justify themselves and their role.

An individual's capacity for trust may influence the degree to which he or she shares information. People who are trusting of others tend to be more forthcoming in sharing information. Individuals operating from a low capacity to trust others will be more inclined to withhold information.

Often leaders are not even aware that information is being withheld. This typically occurs when leaders are dealing with a vast array of issues and are working under tremendous pressure. Furthermore, they often assume that information-sharing channels are open and flowing when in reality they are not. Even though the withholding of information may not have been intended, people experience it as a betrayal, and trust is undermined.

Leaders are employees' best source for honest, accurate, and timely information. Sharing ideas and information with employees builds trust, as well as enhances decision making, productivity, and the bottom line. Through sharing, leadership demonstrates trust in people to manage such information. Armed with a sense of knowing what's what, people are able to focus on performing their jobs with innovation and creativity, rather than expending energy trying to fill in the gaps. The foundation for trust in work relationships is strengthened, and the organization's capacity for trust expands. Withholding information to gain control, power, and perceived job security has the opposite effect and produces significant loss—it undermines trust in your relationship with your employees. The organization's capacity for trust contracts.

Tell the Truth

Do we communicate openly and honestly? Particularly in times of change, people yearn for straightforward communication and need to hear it from their leaders. This means no lying, no exaggerating, no stretching or omitting or "spinning" of the truth. Otherwise, experience shows that when the truth goes by the wayside, trust diminishes. People's natural openness is replaced by cynicism.[4] Regardless of how savvy a leader may be, employees detect when they are receiving anything less than the truth. For them, it is a major betrayal that may take a great deal of time to overcome.

Truth telling is the foundation for trust in an organization, and people deserve nothing short of the truth. Telling the truth sometimes takes courage. And employees look to their leaders to have those "courageous conversations." Especially in times of change, "employees need their leaders to scrupulously and unflinchingly tell the truth—no exceptions, no justifications, no rationalizations."[5] As one health-care finance manager put it, "Leadership means finding a way to be honest at all costs. That is the best way to lead. People want the truth! A good leader finds a way to deliver the hard messages." When persons do not tell the truth, they actually betray themselves. Their sense of trust in themselves is compromised.

"A leader's behavior is crucial in building trust and opening communication."[6] Through their behavior, leaders can facilitate discussion of problems and concerns, and then model a response in a nonjudgmental and engaging way. Having the straight story and accurate information helps employees make better decisions, take the initiative to assume responsibility, be more productive, and make a strong contribution to the organization.

Common in groups, from time to time, are deadlocks in discussions due to tension over differences in viewpoints. When people speak their truth in our interviews, it releases tension and gives others permission to come forth and share their truth. People are more willing to share their thoughts and feelings. This dynamic demonstrates the reciprocal nature of trust. We have to give it to get it!

"There is a rhythm to effective truth telling. To be effective, truth telling needs to fit the flow of the discussion, the moments of openness, and the opportunities that emerge naturally. It weaves its way into the process without trumpets. It simply is, and creates its own power separate from the truth teller. To proceed in any other fashion is to diminish the power of the truth, to draw attention not to the truth but to oneself."[7]

We have often heard employees, at all levels of the organization, express their concerns regarding the willingness of people—including themselves—to tell the truth. "We don't speak the truth at work," a marketing manager said. People tend to withhold the truth or "sugar-coat it to protect the current relationship or to avoid negative repercussions. The truth is too raw; people can't handle it. We are afraid of the truth. We don't trust what others will do with it."

Although avoiding the truth may protect the relationship in the short run, it does damage to the relationship and the trust on which it is built in the long run. "Living in fantasy, although initially pleasant, only serves to erode any real relationship."[8]

Avoiding the truth is a form of betrayal to ourselves and to the people with whom we are in relationship. By not telling the truth, we compromise our sense of trustworthiness to others and to ourselves. The truth, although initially painful, can help people make a better adjustment to a situation, thus expanding the capacity for trust in a relationship.

We recently spent the day with a group of senior executives of one of the largest companies in this country. The purpose of the day was to explore what they, as top leadership, could do to build trusting relationships in their organizations. Through straight talk with one another, a vice president looked at his colleagues and candidly said, "You know, it strikes me that we as a group sit in this room and spend more time talking about how we can put 'spin' on something rather than just telling the truth."

What these executives had become aware of was the time and energy they spent to avoid telling the truth. By adding spin, they were not being honest with their employees or themselves. As this group of executives was able to discover, spinning the truth, no matter how bad the news is, doesn't work. It breaks down a leader's credibility. It creates low trust between the leader and people. Rather than taking the organization a step forward, it takes the organization back several steps.

Admit Mistakes

Do we readily admit mistakes? Do we take responsibility for our mistakes? How leaders deal with mistakes made by themselves or others sets the tone for the rest of the organization and is a key factor in creating communication trust. It does not serve the relationships within an organization to "stonewall" or cover up. When a leader has made a mistake, it really is in his or her own best interest to own up to it. More significant problems are created trying to cover up a mistake. Precious time is wasted and energy and productivity are lost trying to deceive others because of errors made. When energy is focused on covering up mistakes, it saps performance, innovation, and creativity. It costs everyone, in many ways.

Leaders may be reluctant to disclose their mistakes or their concerns and feelings for fear of appearing weak. They may worry that this type of disclosure will compromise their employees' trust in them. However, in all actuality, for leaders at all levels, admitting one's mistakes goes a long way toward rebuilding trust with employees. Employees respect a leader who readily acknowledges his mistakes and makes amends for them. "In admitting when I make a mistake, it sets the tone and creates a safe environment. It shows employees that I am human and that I am vulnerable," said one senior manager in the computer industry. Admitting mistakes demonstrates a strong sense of trust in oneself. Remember, when others perceive that we trust ourselves, they are more inclined to place their trust in us too.

Just as leaders must admit their mistakes, employees must take responsibility for their errors as well. It is important that people who repeatedly make mistakes not hide behind their excuses and abuse your good nature and willingness to forgive.

Give and Receive Constructive Feedback

Do we give constructive feedback in a timely and effective manner? Are we willing and open to receiving feedback without getting defensive? Giving and receiving feedback is a critical factor in creating communication trust.

The president of a large manufacturing firm confided in us that his senior executive team meetings were too cordial. "Everyone is so courteous to one another—too courteous," he remarked. Upon further investigation, we quickly found out that there was a lot of unresolved conflict among the department heads. Because of their reluctance to confront the issues openly and give each other constructive feedback, many issues were not addressed. The managers would talk to the president about their concerns but were unwilling to speak directly to the people involved. The managers hoped the president would intervene and do the talking for them. As the situation continued to go downhill, the level of trust among the senior executive team continued to deteriorate.

Does this sound familiar? Situations like this are not uncommon in organizations where people are unable or unwilling to give each other direct and constructive feedback. As a result, people don't know where they stand, and that undermines the level of trust within the organization.

Trust in ourselves is influenced by feedback. In providing feedback, we are sharing our views, our perceptions, and our experiences of another individual and of the relationship. Positive feedback generates a sense of acceptance that is essential if we are then to take in corrective feedback. Given skillfully, with sensitivity and respect, feedback may open up channels of communication and further the development of trust. In addition, the process of working with feedback, both giving and receiving, provides us with an opportunity to learn more about ourselves as well as others. This increased self-knowledge may expand our capacity for trust and our sense of trustworthiness. When feedback is not a part of organizational life, we are robbed of this opportunity.

Providing constructive feedback sends a message that we are invested in the relationship, that we trust that the individual will pay attention to what we have to say. Sharing information and feelings about another's behavior and performance is critical to maintaining effective working relationships, especially if the other individual's behavior is having a negative effect on performance.

Individuals demonstrate a commitment to a relationship when they express their true thoughts and feelings about each other in a timely and appropriate manner. As one production worker to another on the shop floor of a northeastern manufacturing plant exclaimed, "If you ever get teed off at me, I want you to tell me. I'm a big boy. I can handle it." Or as an office worker exclaimed in a one-on-one communication session, "I don't know how to read you at times, and if I get upset with you, I shut up. That's not good. We need to talk things through with each other as they come up. We need to build on the trust we have had and keep building on it!" Giving each other effective feedback contributes to developing and maintaining trusting relationships that directly affect performance.

One ultimate goal of giving feedback is to improve the capacity of the individuals who are both giving and receiving the feedback. As the individuals develop their own capacities to perform, the capacity of the organization develops.

To give feedback effectively, leaders need to be willing to receive it in return—nondefensively. When receiving feedback, we need to listen to the intent of what people are saying, rather than thinking of a comeback or response. Leaders need to make an effort to avoid becoming defensive and show genuine interest in what they are hearing.[9]

People with a low capacity for trust tend to have difficulty giving and receiving constructive feedback. In giving constructive feedback, if they have unresolved issues with someone with whom they work, the amount and intensity of feedback they give may be out of proportion to a specific occurrence. Individuals with low trust in themselves may generalize about how this situation relates to past mistakes (whether they are similar or not). They may also attempt to project onto others their own feelings of inadequacy and fear, further clouding the issue at hand. Distrust results, which begets more distrust.

In receiving constructive feedback, it may be difficult for some people to trust what needs to be trusted. They may not trust the messenger because of their low capacity to trust. They may not trust that you are genuinely interested in their well-being. Instead of hearing the issues presented, they tend to cloud their perspective by consciously or unconsciously revisiting their past or bringing up prior mistakes they have made. They have difficulty separating the past from the present, possibly because they have unresolved issues.

As a result, their low capacity for self-trust gets projected externally and impedes their ability to develop effective relationships. Issues surrounding their performance don't get resolved but continue to mount. The issues of today get lumped together with the issues of yesterday. These individuals may have difficulty separating who they are from what they do and draw negative conclusions about themselves. "I will never be any good at this," they tell themselves, or "I just can't trust myself in these situations."

Trust develops when people feel comfortable and safe enough to share information regarding one another's behavior or actions without negative repercussions. They trust that they will not suffer the consequences of retaliation because they spoke the truth.

Working constructively with feedback helps develop our capacity to trust—in ourselves, in our views, in our perceptions, and in our experiences. It helps us take our inner voice seriously. From this perspective, it is a gift—to those giving it and to those receiving it. Either way, when done with positive intentions and practiced skill, honest feedback helps us grow, develop, and nurture our capacity to trust.

Maintain Confidentiality

In any kind of relationship, be it with an employee, a coworker or a client, respecting a request for confidentiality is essential to maintaining communication trust. We need to remember that when others have entrusted us with confidential information, we have an obligation to honor that trust, within ourselves and with respect to others.

Do we respect someone's request to maintain the confidentiality of sensitive information? Or do we leak information to a close friend? Violating an agreement of confidentiality is an unabashed betrayal. It is one of the surest and fastest ways to destroy a person's trust in you or your team. And it undermines trust so completely that it may never be overcome.

When trust is low, people fear that their confidential conversations will be spread all over the organization. As one very concerned mid-level manager explained, "We, as a company, can't keep conversations in confidence. As a result, I am afraid to share private information because it gets spread throughout the organization. That is how rumors get started and information gets distorted."

How do we deal with this kind of behavior? Such a breach of trust needs to be confronted with candor, respect, and sensitivity. Confronting others when there has been a breach of confidentiality is necessary if there is to be any kind of trusting relationship in the future. The following illustrates how one colleague addressed a breach of confidentiality with another: "I bring myself to you with the highest integrity and confidentiality. I asked you on Monday to maintain confidence about X. After our conversation, I heard that you shared that information with others. I expect from you the same high degree of integrity and confidentiality that I bring to you. If I have a conversation with you in confidence, I expect you to keep it. Are we in agreement?"

Having this kind of conversation lets the other party know that you know what has happened. It establishes a clear boundary and sets explicit expectations (contractual trust) regarding future communication between the two of you. If we fail to address this kind of behavior, animosity and distrust result in our relationship with others. Left unaddressed, it can diminish any relationship. If this behavior proliferates in the workplace, it can destroy all trust and cripple the organization's performance.

Speak with Good Purpose

Do we gossip about fellow employees behind their backs? Or if we have a concern or issue with an individual, do we speak directly to the person? When individuals speak with good purpose, they speak constructively and affirmatively and stand up for each other. Conversely, when workers gossip, criticize, and shun other workers, they destroy trust between individuals, within a team, and throughout an organization. The consequences are devastating to morale and to performance. In such work climates, the organization's capacity to trust severely diminishes. "We talk about each other behind each other's backs," admitted one supervisor in the electronics industry. "When someone has an issue with another, we don't speak directly to that person but blab it all over the lunchroom. Backbiting is rampant around here!"

Do we share what is on our mind clearly and freely, or do we use insinuating remarks or slighting digs to convey our thoughts indirectly? When individuals are called to task for indirect remarks, do they take responsibility or hide behind a white lie: "Oh, I was only joking. Don't be so sensitive!" When colleagues engage in dishonest communication by not saying what they mean openly and directly, they misrepresent the reality of their feelings. In so doing, they do harm to their relationships. This is a betrayal to themselves and others. The cost is their trustworthiness. Soon other people will not trust them and will be guarded around them. They will withhold information about themselves for fear of being hurt or treated disrespectfully.

When we do not speak with good purpose, we betray our inner sense of ourselves. When we hide behind inappropriate humor and sarcasm, we betray our true voice, we betray what we have that really needs to be said and shared. The price we pay is the cost of a trusting relationship.

Leaders need to counter unfair criticism head on. Regarding gossiping and backbiting, leaders need to make it explicitly clear that engaging in such behavior is inappropriate, unprofessional, and intolerable in the workplace. Speaking out against gossip will earn you respect and trust with your employees.

When we share information, tell the truth, admit mistakes, use feedback constructively, maintain confidentiality, and speak with good purpose, we build communication trust. Communication trust helps us create and maintain supportive working relationships.

How Communication Trust Builds Relationships

People create relationships for all kinds of reasons. The most basic is need. Relationships are a fundamental human need. "Good working relationships are a primary way to get things done, as long as the relationships are genuine and authentic."[10] Betrayal occurs when relationships are used for the purpose of exploiting another person to serve ourselves.

A number of leaders we interviewed work very hard to break down barriers and open communication with people. They found that people welcome the opportunity to experience a leader's humanness. People want to see the different aspects of you as a leader. Seeing you as a human being helps open up communication between you and them. They see you as approachable.

A leader's credibility unfolds through the development of trusting relationships. Trust develops through active engagement and participation with others. Enter into meaningful dialogue with your people. They want it! Find out what matters to them. Engage them in conversation about matters important to you and them. Let them hear and see what is on your mind.

Relationships develop through leaders' demonstrating a strong sense of trust in their people. The practice of communication trust helps a leader understand people better. A leader can't take an organization single-handedly where it needs to go. The leader has to be able to count on effective relationships with people and help them learn to enhance their contribution to the organization. Inclusion and involvement need to become integral to their daily operating style. Trust and fairness are reinforced by words and actions. "Trust is a delicate property of human relationships. It is influenced far more by actions than by words. It takes a long time to build, but it can be destroyed very quickly. Even a single action, perhaps misunderstood, can have powerful effects."[11]

A subtle yet common way leaders betray employees is by not practicing the behaviors of communication trust. Understanding people means recognizing the importance and validity of their need for communication. Trust develops between leaders and their people when they understand that you care and are there to support them—to take risks and to fulfill their responsibilities. Communication trust contributes to the development of safe and productive work environments where an individual's capacity to trust in self and others increases and the organization's capacity to perform expands.

IDEAS IN ACTION

Here we present questions and an exercise leaders can consider in building and maintaining communication trust with their people. The questions may also be used by a leader or facilitator to open communication between individuals on a team.

Questions to Consider

Reflect on the following questions, and record your thoughts.

1. Where in your personal and work life do you experience high levels of communication trust? What happens when you experience a low level of communication trust?

2. How willingly do you share information with others? Do you receive the information you need? What happens to your communication trust when you don't? What can you do in the future to share information at a high level and encourage others to share with you?

3. Do others tell you the truth? What happens to your level of trust when you question the truthfulness of others? What can you do to encourage more truth telling both by yourself and by others?

4. Are you willing to admit your mistakes? What happens when you do admit mistakes? What do you do when others admit their mistakes? What can you do to support the admission of mistakes within your organization?

5. How do giving and receiving constructive feedback contribute to communication trust in your organization? In what ways have you experienced reductions in communication trust? What can you do in the future to encourage constructive feedback?

6. How do you decide what to share and what to hold back? How do you balance this behavior with the need to share information discussed previously?

7. How do people speak of each other in your organization? Do they speak respectfully of others, or is there a lot of gossiping and backbiting? What can you do to promote speaking with good purpose in your organization?

Application Exercise

The following exercise is intended to facilitate communication trust within a group or team.

One-on-One Communication Meetings. This process is effective in dealing with interpersonal issues that impede communication and performance within a group. Construct a matrix of all the participants in the group so that every person has an opportunity to have a one-on-one meeting with everyone else. Set up the meetings for one to two hours. (Refer to the communication matrix in the following illustration as a sample.) Have participants speak candidly to one another regarding how they interact and work together. You may use the following sentences to add structure to the meeting. Have each person reflect on these in preparation for the meetings with each of their teammates.

- What I appreciate about you is . . .
- What works in our relationship is . . .
- What doesn't work in our relationship is . . .
- What I need from you is . . .
- Let's brainstorm together ways in which we can work together better.

This exercise works with groups as small as four individuals or as large as twelve. For larger groups, you might want to subdivide the participants into subgroups to expedite the process.

Communication Matrix

__PURPOSE__: To facilitate the logistics of everyone participating in this communication exercise

__PARTICIPANTS__:
    1. Harry   5. Rachel
    2. Maria   6. Jackson
    3. Carlos   7. Joanne
    4. Lee

__PROCESS__: The participants will speak to each other in the prescribed rounds during the following weeks:

	May 7–9	May 12–16		May 19–23		May 26–30	
Rounds	**1**	**2**	**3**	**4**	**5**	**6**	**7**
Participants	1 ↔ 7	1 ↔ 6	1 ↔ 5	1 ↔ 4	1 ↔ 3	1 ↔ 2	2 ↔ 7
	2 ↔ 6	2 ↔ 5	2 ↔ 4	2 ↔ 3	6 ↔ 5	6 ↔ 4	6 ↔ 3
	3 ↔ 5	3 ↔ 4	7 ↔ 6	7 ↔ 5	7 ↔ 4	7 ↔ 3	5 ↔ 4

__EXAMPLE__:
During the week of May 7–9, the following people talk with each other:

    Harry and Joanne
    Maria and Jackson
    Carlos and Rachel

If there is low trust or antagonism within the group, it is advisable to have these sessions facilitated by a skilled facilitator who does not have a relationship with any of the participants. It is important to conduct the sessions in a confined time frame to achieve optimum results. We strongly encourage that team members contract with one another before the sessions start to keep these conversations confidential. (Establish working agreements ahead of time to ensure the psychological safety of the participants.)

8

COMPETENCE TRUST

So trust people, they are capable of greatness.
STANISLAW LEM

In this chapter, you will learn about:

- A definition of Competence Trust
- The nature of Competence Trust
- Behaviors that foster Competence Trust
- A comparison of disappointment and betrayal

A DEFINITION OF COMPETENCE TRUST

Competence trust involves respecting people's knowledge, skills and abilities, and judgment, involving others and seeking their input, and helping people learn skills. How we practice these behaviors demonstrates our willingness to trust the capability of ourselves and others. Therefore, we can characterize competence trust as "trust of capability" (see Figure 5C).

People's sense of personal worth is often measured by their competence in their jobs. Naturally, people are then motivated to develop competence in what they do and how they do it. Most people want and need to know they make a difference and contribute to the overall good of the

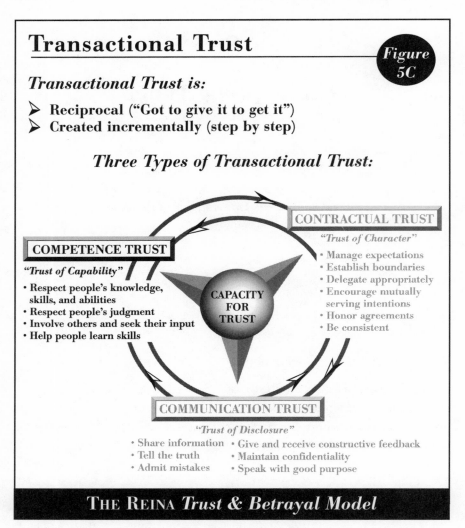

Figure 5C   The Competence Form of Transactional Trust

organization. It is important for leaders to be aware of this fundamental need in people and help people apply their abilities in meaningful ways to meet business challenges. Acting in this way, leaders not only honor their relationships with their employees but also contribute to the overall health of their business.

THE NATURE OF COMPETENCE TRUST

Broadly speaking, competence trust refers to the ability to do what is needed and the capacity to interact effectively with others.[1] Narrowly speaking, it means being able to rely on someone to complete a specific task properly. Competence trust is an absolute requirement for work to get done in an organization, whether that work is a specific task or a more complex combination of activities. People count on each other to be able to do their jobs.

Quite often when we think of competence in the workplace, we think of the formal mechanisms we have become dependent on to develop our workforce. We may think of personnel policies aimed at tracking people's abilities and performance. We think of formal training programs designed to teach us "what we need to know." However, competence is more than education and training programs. It is more than hiring and promotion policies. It is more than information, tools, and technology, important as they are. Competence is not just the exclusive preserve of the human resource department; it is everybody's business—an organizational state of mind.[2]

An important component of competence trust is the ability of individuals to deal effectively with the demands and expectations placed on them by leadership and the organization. This ability relates to the skill, knowledge, attitude, behavior, confidence, and experience aimed at fulfilling the responsibilities associated with defined roles and holding oneself accountable. Competence trust is found where leaders and employees learn from one another, where they are learning from their customers, suppliers, and competitors. This happens when communication trust is strong; where information exchange is easy and open—up, down, across, inside, and outside the organization; where leaders and employees are open to new thoughts, approaches, methods, procedures, and policies.[3]

You know competence trust when you experience it. You see it, feel it, and hear it. Requests for information are responded to swiftly; assistance with a complicated project is provided without hesitation; questions or concerns regarding an issue are answered directly and candidly. Competence trust starts and finishes with knowledgeable people who are highly responsible, hold themselves accountable, are committed to continuous improvement, and are aligned with the objectives and needs of their organization.

Behaviors That Foster Competence Trust

There are a number of behaviors that leaders can practice in order to build and maintain competence trust in their organizations.

Respect People's Knowledge, Skills, and Abilities

Do we respect our employees' abilities to do their jobs? Do we give them the resources, authority, and responsibility they need to get their work done right?

Matt, a competent engineer, was promoted to a managerial position. For years he enjoyed the hands-on fieldwork of his job. He liked having complete control of the projects assigned to him. Now as manager, he has added administrative functions to his responsibilities. Matt doesn't have time for hands-on contact with the projects for which he is responsible, but he wishes he did. He is having a hard time delegating to his employees. He wants to delegate but has concerns about their abilities, and he is not taking the time to train them. When he does delegate projects, he is constantly looking over their shoulder, telling them what to do.

Do you trust in people's competence to do the task, to get the job done? Respecting people's knowledge, skills, and abilities is reflected in a willingness to allow people to use their talents to accomplish goals. It is important to be aware of a need to control, if you have one, and the impact of your attempts at controlling employees instead of trusting them. The more you trust them, the less need there is for control.

Matt's challenge to balance his own need to have hands-on contact while allowing his people to do their jobs and to grow in those jobs is shared by many managers. To keep people motivated, it is the leader's role to challenge them and provide opportunities for people to increase their skills and knowledge.

As you develop your people, they demonstrate your trust in their capabilities. You are actually investing in them and the relationship, and there are rewards. In your effort to invest in the development of your people's competence, you are in turn developing in your own. As they grow and develop, so do you. As they assume additional responsibilities, you further explore professional interests and further develop your competence as a mentor.

People with a limited capacity for trust in themselves may not view themselves as competent. They may not be aware of their potential. When you see the potential in people, it allows you to trust in their potential competence. You provide them with a remarkable gift. For when you trust in them, you open the door for them to trust in themselves, for them to discover themselves further. With this foundation in place, and with support and guidance, people flourish. Giving employees freedom and flexibility within parameters and trusting them to do their jobs pays dividends—to you, to them, and to the organization. It enables them to accomplish more than they may ever have expected. Their competence is enriched, and their capacity for trust expands.

When leaders trust in employees' competence instead of micromanaging, they give their employees the freedom and latitude to do their jobs. Under these circumstances, trust is more than reciprocated. Employees will usually exceed the leader's expectations. "A while back," a manager with a large consulting firm said, "I gave a junior team member the task of making a proposal presentation to a prospective client. Not being fully aware of his abilities, I took a risk; it took some trust. It was a long shot. However, the junior team member was highly motivated and did a lot of work in preparation for the event. He made a great presentation, and we got the contract. He actually exceeded my expectations and hopes. It took a leap of faith on my part." This leader gave trust and was not disappointed in return. He, the junior team member, and the organization benefited.

But what about the time when it doesn't work out, when you are trusting your employee with a major project and he or she drops the ball? How should you handle the situation? Obviously, each situation must be reviewed individually. However, you need to assess each situation "with open eyes" and determine whom you can trust with what. You need to listen to yourself and follow your intuition.

Carlos, vice president and comptroller for a dynamic restaurant group known for excellence, shares a hard lesson he learned. "Having competence trust is not blind trust—you've got to follow your intuition. I allowed Leonard, who was outwardly very confident, to 'snow' me. Leonard's confidence overshadowed a slipshod approach to his books. I trusted him, but I should have followed my instincts. He didn't perform up to my expectations." By the time Carlos realized Leonard was not performing up to par, it was almost too late. The books were due, and Carlos's appointee had failed to deliver. Carlos reflects, "The lesson for me is 'do not be afraid to confront.' A lot of external distractions clouded my intuition. Because of my trust in this employee, I made an assumption, that Leonard should know how to do this closing. His assertiveness and confidence I mistook for competence. I needed to trust my intuition."

This story illustrates the hard lesson we all need to learn, some of us time and time again: when we don't listen to our inner voice, we betray ourselves.

Trusting in your own competence is directly related to the need to trust your intuition. Your beliefs about your abilities have a profound effect on those abilities.[4] If you believe you have the competence and the confidence to meet certain goals for yourself, that belief will influence your success.

Your readiness to trust in your competence starts with your capacity to trust in yourself. Your capacity to trust influences how trusting you are of yourself and how trusting you are of others. Your capacity to trust influences your beliefs and perceptions about yourself and others. "If I see myself as trustworthy, I project that," a health-care human resource manager observed. "My self-concept and worldview determine how trustingly I view others."

Risk taking, essential to business success, is directly related to trust in our own competence. Trust in our competence influences our thoughts regarding our ability to keep up with the changing demands of our jobs. We question, "Can I keep up? Can I learn the new system? Do I have what it takes?" In low-trust work environments, people are reluctant to take risks and admit mistakes for fear of looking incompetent. Working in this type of environment, over time, an individual may begin to doubt or question their own competence.

Ray was his own worst critic. He was afraid of taking a risk for fear of making a mistake. When he did make a mistake, he would repeatedly beat up on himself. He didn't want to let the team down, yet his fear of letting the team down paralyzed his performance. He was so focused on the fear—in a way, he was trusting his fear instead of trusting himself—that he continued to fail. His supervisor asked if he could coach Ray, and Ray acquiesced. "I urged him to stay in the present," his supervisor said, "to focus on the objectives, not on the obstacles, and to use the help of his teammates." As he began to focus on the present and ask for help from his teammates, he started to make some progress. He started to trust himself and his teammates more—though not without occasional slip-ups. Ultimately, he was successful in accomplishing one major task and then another and another. He started to gain a sense of success and then pride in following through and accomplishing his goals. That was over a year ago. Ray continues to grow, step by step, learning more about himself, trusting more in himself. His confidence in his competence grows each day.

For the first time in his life, somebody took the time and patience to work with Ray. As a result of his supervisor's efforts, Ray began to blossom.

Respect People's Judgment

"It is not that I don't trust his integrity—I don't trust his judgment!" Sound familiar? Do we allow employees the freedom and flexibility to make decisions? Respecting people's judgment in the workplace means giving people a chance to use their judgment to make decisions that affect their work.

Sometimes you may not have prior experience to judge an employee's competence, to assess whether you can trust that person's judgment. This is especially the case in a relatively new relationship, as with new employees or perhaps with experienced employees working on new projects. In these times, you must use your best judgment and trust in that judgment. When you make a judgment call, it is critical that you empower employees to make decisions within the scope of their responsibilities, to the best of their ability without encumbering them with your insecurities. Drawing on your judgment to trust their competence positions them to make a full contribution, to learn, grow, and further develop their competence. As Jack Welch said, "Any company that's going to make it . . . has got to find a way to engage the mind of every single employee. If you're not thinking all the time about making every person more valuable, you don't have a chance. What's the alternative? Wasted minds? Uninvolved people? A labor force that's angry or bored? That doesn't make sense."[5]

Involve Others and Seek Their Input

Think of an occasion when someone asked for your advice or opinion on a matter. How did it feel? Pretty good? When you involve or seek the involvement of others, it demonstrates your trust in their competence.

Do you involve others in planning, decision making, and problem solving related to the scope of their job responsibility and your stated expectations of their performance? Do you allow your employees to discuss and even challenge your decisions with the end goal of achieving what is best for the organization? When employees feel safe enough to challenge your decisions (in appropriate and respectful ways), this is an indication of the trust that exists in the relationship. Your willingness to engage your employees in dialogue to seek their views and to explore possible alternatives will ultimately further develop trusting relationships and produce the best results for the organization.

"Allow employees to take ownership and have pride in their work," advised a manufacturing vice president. "Challenge their thought processes. Give employees the stimulus to do things." When you seek out the input of others, you demonstrate your trust in their competence. In return, you gain from their advice and enhance the trust between you and them. Trusting in people's ability deepens their sense of ownership and accomplishment in their work. Furthermore, a foundation of trust in the relationship forms. Their capacity to trust in themselves and your capacity to trust in yourself grows.

We often hear employees voice resignation and frustration about not having input. From factory floors to high-rise offices, we hear employees say, "Either they don't trust us or they figure we don't have anything to contribute, so they don't ask us" or "Nobody ever asks me what I think." When employees' ideas have not been solicited, or worse yet, when they have been solicited but their ideas are not valued, people feel betrayed. In not recognizing or valuing people's competence, actual or potential, a leader betrays what the individual has to offer. It is a betrayal of both the individual and the organization: the individual is cut off from the opportunity to make a full contribution, and the organization is robbed of that individual's full talent. What a waste of human talent, a loss of human motivation and unachieved potential!

Help People Learn Skills

"It is not what employees know but what they come to know that is important."[6] Investing in people is a powerful way to demonstrate your trust in their capacity to develop their competence. As mentors, leaders need to find out about what motivates people and work with them to develop their capacity and potential. Doing so enhances the development of trust in their own competence and hence their performance. Trust in leaders grows when employees are supported in gaining relevant knowledge and skills and in applying that knowledge and those skills on the job.

During our interviews with senior executives, they all spoke of the changing work contract. They spoke of the struggle they face regarding what they can and cannot guarantee their employees. Long-term job security no longer exists. Assisting their employees to develop competence is one aspect many leaders said they could guarantee. One senior manager at corporate headquarters of a large chemical manufacturing company tells his employees, "I can't guarantee you job security, but I can guarantee that I will try my hardest to make you all you can be." B. J. Smith, manager of Duke Power's workforce planning, echoes this sentiment: "There is no such thing as job security anymore. I tell people the only form of job security I can give them is training in a broader array of skills than they have now. From now on, they have to prepare to help themselves."[7]

Although leaders may not be able to guarantee jobs for life, they can make a commitment to develop their people. Leaders who do make that commitment make a wide array of developmental tools available. People may choose from a variety of training programs; they may have the opportunity to attend outside workshops or conferences or visit other organizations to observe their methods and practices. Many leaders provide employees with the flexibility to continue their formal education or to experience the assistance of a professional coach. A leader may ask an individual to head up a special project or provide a promotional opportunity as a further means of developing the person's skills and experience.

Leaders have an obligation to develop employees, and those employees, in return, have an obligation to pursue their own growth and development. "Leaders need to get their people to be more empowered," said one chemical plant manager. "To do so, individuals need to take responsibility for their own person. They need to be in touch with themselves and their needs. They need to make choices (with eyes wide open) to get their needs met versus blindly trusting in the organizations [in which they work] to get their needs met." When people see others highly involved in their own personal development, they tend to be more trusting of their competence.

When leaders trust in their people's competence, they influence and empower their employees to go beyond current beliefs about their personal limitations. Their capacity for trust in themselves and others expands. The development of people's competence can be thrilling and exciting for all involved. It can also be quite challenging. Leaders and employees alike know that to develop the capacity of their organizations, there must be opportunities to stretch and grow. However, leaders and employees often find themselves in a catch-22 situation. They find themselves in a place where they become driven by day-to-day pressures and demands and therefore feel as though they "can't afford the time" to invest in development. Underutilization of talent and potential is often the result.

A leader's ability to develop the competence of employees and thereby develop the capacity of the organization is critical to the organization's maintaining a competitive edge. Effective leaders create environments where people are not afraid to take risks and tackle new areas.

DILBERT reprinted by permission of United Feature Syndicate, Inc.

They create the psychological as well as the physical safety for people to stretch themselves to accomplish business objectives. Within these safe boundaries, people are able to focus on what they were hired to do: produce products and services and satisfy customers. "Create the space so that people can find out for themselves and learn. They may not get it right the first time, but they will get there," said a senior manager for an international chemical company. People need the freedom and the flexibility to learn from their mistakes. People's trust in their competence and in their leaders grows. Conversely, when the organizational environment does not support people's learning from their mistakes, competence trust in themselves and their leaders dwindles.

The *Dilbert* cartoon above illustrates the cost of not allowing people to make mistakes and learn from them.

When there is fear in the workplace, people's capacity for trust contracts. They are unwilling or, as in the *Dilbert* cartoon, unable to exercise their given talents and realize their performance potential. People working under these conditions are hindered or, in this case, frozen by fear.

After working in such an environment for some time, people's capacity for trust in themselves declines. Their willingness to be creative and innovative shuts down. These people feel betrayed by the organization in which they work. Their competence trust in themselves diminishes.

In dealing with these challenges, it is easy to get discouraged. Leaders, however, cannot give up on people or themselves when disappointed in performance. If someone is not living up to performance expectations, it is a leader's job to continue to nurture the person's potential and to trust in the person's ability. Being an effective leader means being able to reach out to each individual. It is important to be able to feed upon people's strengths and work with their weaknesses while the dynamics are constantly changing.[8] It is about trusting where they are and trusting where they have the potential to be.

A COMPARISON OF DISAPPOINTMENT AND BETRAYAL

It is difficult to betray trust relative to competence in performing a job. If a person honestly tries but fails to accomplish a task because of a lack of skills or aptitude, it may be a disappointment or a failure, but it is not an intentional betrayal. "I asked you to do X; you gave it your best effort but came up short. I am disappointed." If, however, the individual did have the ability but chose not to use that talent, it is a betrayal. Knowingly failing to meet expectations is an intentional breach of contractual trust.

Leaders may be disappointed, even frustrated, by an employee's performance, but they must continue to provide support. Support is necessary for people to develop. Competence trust is earned incrementally and is "built behaviorally." The leader's daily actions of respecting employee's abilities and judgment, involving them in planning and decision making, and helping them learn new skills develop their capacity to contribute as employees, our capacity as leaders, and the organization's capacity to perform. The more we trust in our employees, the more trust they have in us.

We can change our capacity for trust in our own competence. That is, we can change our basic readiness and willingness to trust ourselves in how we approach solving problems, how we approach learning. Learning new ways of doing and, more important, new ways of being may require us to unlearn old habits, thoughts, and perspectives that no longer serve us well. It may require us to relearn or reframe our learning, and it starts with self-reflection.

The process of self-reflection or self-inquiry helps you shift your perspective and take more responsibility for your circumstances in your life and perhaps influence their outcomes. The Ideas in Action section at the end of this chapter provides questions to aid in your self-reflection.

The old Chinese proverb is as true today as ever: "If you want one year of prosperity, grow grain. If you want ten years of prosperity, grow trees. If you want one hundred years of prosperity, grow people."

IDEAS IN ACTION

Here we provide questions and exercises that leaders can use in building and maintaining competence trust with their people. The questions may also be used by a leader or facilitator to enhance competence trust between individuals on a team.

Questions to Consider

Reflect on the following questions, and record your thoughts.

1. Where in your personal and work life do you experience high levels of competence trust in yourself? In others?
2. Do you have appreciation for your own knowledge, skills, and abilities? What happens when you feel less trust in your own or someone else's competence?
3. Are you reluctant to give others a chance to perform because you fear their failure? How do those decisions affect your workload? How might you help create situations where they have a much better chance of succeeding?
4. What action might you take to support the confidence you already have or actually increase your sense of your own competence?
5. Do you respect other people's judgment? Do you let others make decisions, or do you assume that no one can make decisions as good as yours? How does this affect your trust in the competence of others?

6. How do you involve others in matters that affect them? In what ways do you seek their input? When you do, what is the effect on your trust in their competence? On their trust in their own competence?
7. In what ways do you develop your own capabilities? What actions do you take that help others develop their own capacities? What might you do differently in the future to enhance this even more?

Application Exercises

The following exercises are intended to facilitate competence trust in a group or team.

A. *Each One Teach One.* This is a method of cross-training in which people proficient or experienced in certain skills contract with their coworkers to teach them skills they need. This approach is also useful when people go to outside training and come back and train their peers on the basis of what they learned. Teaching others what we learn challenges us to "know our stuff" by helping us internalize and integrate our learning. In addition, it encourages sharing of information and expertise that builds competence trust and support in each other while developing the capacity of the team. It also helps maximize the training dollar investment.

Instructions:
1. The next time you attend a training session, contract to teach what you learned to a coworker who did not attend the session.
2. After completion of the training, review the material covered and prepare an outline of the key knowledge and skills learned.
3. Set up blocks of uninterrupted time to share what you learned with your coworker. Check for clarity and understanding as you proceed through the process.
4. Brainstorm ways each of you can support each other in applying the new knowledge on the job.

B. *Creating Learning Contracts.* Employing learning contracts with people in training programs or involved in on-the-job training helps ensure application of skills and learning. The following illustration is a sample matrix of questions people address prior to engaging in a specific learning process. It formally outlines skills and knowledge they want or need to learn to do their current job or take on additional responsibilities, resources they will use to acquire the skills and knowledge, projected dates to learn skills or have a basic understanding of the knowledge, and application of learning.

Instructions:

1. Use the Learning Contract below as a tool for professional development.
2. After an employee returns from training, have them fill out the form and meet with them to discuss their learning plans.
3. Follow-up with the employee to support them in their learning process.

Learning Contract

Name: _____

JOB SPECIFIC SKILLS AND KNOWLEDGE	RESOURCES NEEDED	PROJECTED DATE	APPLICATION OF LEARNING
What I would like or need to learn to do my current job or take on additional responsibilities	*How I will learn or acquire the skills and knowledge*	*When I will have a basic grasp of the knowledge and skills*	*How I will demonstrate what I've learned on the job*
1.	1.	1.	1.
2.	2.	2.	2.
3.	3.	3.	3.

Signature: _____ **Date:** _____

9

REBUILDING TRUST IN TEAMS

*Trust building is a team's foundation; it is
critical to all other task issues.*
ALLAN DREXLER, DAVID SIBBETT, AND RUSSELL FORRESTER

In this chapter, you will learn about:

• The importance of trust to team effectiveness
• Applying the Reina Trust & Betrayal Model to build trust in teams

*Your heart is pounding. Your stomach is in knots. The tension
in the room is so thick, you need a chainsaw to cut it. The
team must reach resolution on a key initiative. The boss is presenting
his views on the topic, and everyone in the room is nodding in agreement. Yet twenty-five minutes ago at the water cooler, these same people
were complaining that it was a "stupid idea," that it would never work.
The boss finishes his presentation and asks the group, "So what do you
think?" Team members anxiously shift in their seats, look around the
room, avoid eye contact with each other. Everyone is quiet. Meanwhile,
the voice inside your head is screaming, "Will somebody please say
something!" You begin speaking only to clamp shut again, succumbing
to the other voice inside your head, which says, "Don't do it. It's not
safe. What if the boss doesn't like what you say and retaliates?" A similar*

message is being played in the heads of every individual around the
table. "I am not going to speak. You do it! I'm not taking
any chances."[1]

Have you experienced a team meeting like this? It is a far too common scenario. When there is insufficient trust within a team, members do not share openly. Instead, they have private conversations around the water cooler with the few people they trust. Or ideas and concerns get buried deep under cynicism and resentment. As a result, team members feel bad about the team, and the team's effectiveness suffers.

THE IMPORTANCE OF TRUST TO TEAM EFFECTIVENESS

People come to teams with a range of expectations and emotions. These expectations and emotions often reflect previous experiences. Some of our expectations concern how safe we expect the team to be. Many of our emotions are associated with those expectations.

Perhaps you have had a positive team experience where members treated one another with dignity and respect and where people shared information and views with one another openly, acknowledging what each had to offer. Your team may have had a strong foundation of trust that carried it through the challenging times. The team felt good about what it accomplished.

Or perhaps your team experience was one in which people were not treated with dignity and respect. Perhaps people did not follow through on their commitments and failed to complete team assignments. Perhaps members just stopped showing up for meetings. You may have experienced having your ideas "put down" before you were able to express them fully. You may have felt the pain of no trust and the loss of any hope that it could be built.

Trust in relationships is something for which we all yearn. It is a fundamental human need. Since teams are constituted on relationships, it comes as no surprise that team effectiveness is largely dependent on a foundation of trust. Trust is the glue that binds team members together. It helps foster a sense of belonging and influences members' willingness to communicate openly, commit to the team's goals, take risks, and support one another.

Many leaders realize that teams can be effective in helping organizations meet their objectives and adapt to change. As a result, teams are widely used in organizations today. They are not always successful, however. Often a lack of trust prevents teams from developing to their fullest and most effective extent.

Being a member of a team represents a risk for some people. Some people may have had no prior experience being a member of a team. Or they may never have been on a team like the one they have been asked to join. Worse, they may have had a negative team experience. In this chapter, we will explore how the three forms of *transactional trust* can be used to strengthen existing trust and rebuild trust after betrayal. A sampling of the behaviors under each form of transactional trust will be examined to illustrate how they are experienced in teams.

CONTRACTUAL TRUST IN TEAMS

Manage Expectations and Establish Boundaries

"What is expected of me to be a member of this team? Can I do what is expected of me? Will team members accept me?" At the onset of a team's work, team members have a strong need to know what is expected of them and what they may expect in return. Whereas the team's purpose defines the reason for the team's existence, expectations define the objectives for the team's members. Explicit expectations also define team boundaries, roles, and responsibilities. Therefore, understanding expectations is crucial to the formation of a team and the development of trust within that team.

When trust is high, team members feel they are "in the know." Trust is high because team members have discussed their expectations and understand them. Members feel they are in the know because they took the time to clarify their expectations and achieve agreement and alignment at the outset.

When expectations are not clear, team members may feel confused, anxious, and vulnerable. When the purpose of the team has not been clearly established, team members have difficulty being aligned toward the same objectives.

The important thing is to create alignment so that team members can rally behind the same objectives and trust that all members are working toward the same goals. The following practices work well. Quarterly planning sessions help members get a clear idea of the direction in which they need to head. Daily ten-minute stand-up meetings allow people to manage their day-to-day work, announce intentions, identify needs, and make requests of each other. Monthly progress reviews allow people to take stock of their accomplishments and challenges to be overcome. These can be done in person with teams at the same site or on-line with virtual or geographically dispersed teams.

Honor Agreements

Members often have a series of questions on their minds regarding what is acceptable team behavior: "How will decisions be made? Will I have access to information? Is it OK occasionally to miss a meeting to handle other obligations? Is it OK to say, 'I don't know'?" People further question how meetings will be facilitated and how the team will work together.

Working agreements make explicit how team members would like to work together. Under these agreements, team members set out a contract regarding how they will behave. Many groups have ground rules or team charters that govern team member behavior both at meetings and in other settings. These working agreements help create an environment of predictability and trust within the team. As with any agreement, their power comes alive when the words are taken off the pages and put into practice, lived on a daily basis. Honoring these agreements means that team members are willing to be accountable for their actions. When members honor their agreements, large or small, it strengthens trust within the team.

Conversely, "when we don't do as we say, when we don't keep our agreements or renegotiate broken agreements, it erodes trust," the vice president of a pharmaceutical company noted. Failure to show up for meetings on time, to provide information as promised, or to complete an assignment are examples of team members not honoring their agreements. Such failures are betrayals—of member's obligations and their word.

When this behavior becomes a pattern, people are no longer able trust any member's promise: "He said he would be here, but he never shows up, so let's move on." "She said she would fax the expense breakdown, but she has said that before and not delivered. Where else can we get it?"

When team members ask for help and don't get it, it breaks trust. Elaine may not have intended to hurt the team by not showing up, but her teammates experience her behavior as a betrayal nonetheless. There is a tremendous price when we do not honor our commitments: we compromise our trustworthiness in the eyes of others and ourselves.

Encourage Mutually Serving Intentions

When team members encourage mutually serving intentions rather than operate with hidden agendas, they jointly support each other in being successful. As a result, trust is nurtured. Unfortunately, hidden agendas are often a part of a team's life. They occur for a variety of reasons. They occur when individuals do not fully disclose their interests and needs and then work to meet them covertly. They may take many different forms. Team members may withhold information, thinking that this self-serving action will help them maintain power and look like experts as they position themselves for promotion.

Hidden agendas break down trust and lead to betrayal, but they arise only when there is insufficient trust in the first place. In a situation of trust, people can talk openly about their expectations, intentions, hopes, and fears. They may even enlist group members to help them. Group members feel free to say no without fear that some other member will try to circumvent their decisions.

However, when trust is low and team members operate with hidden agendas, it destroys trust within teams at any level of the organization.

The top-management team of a small hospital system was having difficulty operating effectively as a team. The president was aware that there was a low level of trust within the team, but he did not know why.

In our work with the team, we learned that his relationship with the CFO carried a hidden agenda that compromised the level of trust within the team and in him. The CFO was highly competent, but she was a tyrant in the way she treated her coworkers. She would verbally attack her colleagues on issues during team meetings, rather than speak to them constructively in private. She was condescending and often abrasive. The other team members were unwilling to confront her for fear of retaliation. They were dismayed that the president allowed this behavior to continue.

Upon further investigation, we discovered his hidden agenda. He used the CFO to do his "dirty work" for him. The president did not want to come across as the bad guy in delivering the tough messages to his team. So he had the CFO confront members with his issues. Over time, the team all but shut down, information flow decreased, and trust "dropped through the floor." The president lost all trust and credibility in the eyes of his key people. Eventually, he was asked to resign. The CFO left a short time after.

The president's self-serving actions destroyed contractual trust within the team. To help this team heal and move on, team members first needed to talk about what they went through in recent years. The pain they felt needed to be acknowledged, and their feelings needed to surface. Working with the team, we first created a safe environment for honest dialogue to happen. To begin the process, we used the Seven Steps for Healing from Betrayal as a framework to guide discussions. After a number of sessions, team members were able to reframe their experiences and take responsibility for the parts they each had played. Then we used the three forms of transactional trust to identify behaviors that had hindered trust within the team and to strategize actions to support the level of trust they wanted. During the following two years, the team would periodically pull out the Reina Trust & Betrayal Model to monitor and evaluate its progress.

COMMUNICATION TRUST IN TEAMS

Team members have a strong need to be able to communicate openly with one another. They need to feel free to ask questions, honestly say what is on their minds, challenge assumptions, raise issues, or simply say they don't understand something and ask for help. Only in a trusting environment will people feel free to relate to one another in this way.

Share Information

When team members do not share information, it significantly hinders the development of trust on a team. This is an issue many teams face. When a team member withholds information, that behavior is perceived as self-serving, and the person's trustworthiness and commitment to the team are called into question.

When team members share information, it is powerful. It contributes to the learning of individuals, as well as the team. When information is not shared, performance suffers. A supervisor in a health-care system shares her observations regarding the power of information:

> One of the teams openly shared the information they were learning in class. In fact, the trainees scheduled periodic feedback sessions with their teammates not attending the classes to share what they learned. In addition to enhancing each other's knowledge, the trainees became consultants and coaches for each other back on the job. As a result, the free exchange between the trainees and the other team members enhanced the cohesiveness, trust, and performance of the entire team.
>
> The other team tried to enhance performance through competition. They viewed information as power, so instead of sharing information, they withheld it. Doors closed (literally), and people shut down. These behaviors led to a secretive and "cutthroat" working environment. As a result, the level of trust and performance within this team declined.

The team that shared information outperformed the one that withheld it. The first team strengthened not only communication trust among its members but contractual trust and competence trust as well. When team members returned from each training session, they kept their agreements and built contractual trust in coaching each other. Furthermore, this enhanced the skills of each team member and developed competence trust in one another.

Open communication was desperately needed to turn the other team around. Because trust was so low, we started with an assessment to identify the issues that were interfering with the team's effectiveness and its members' ability to trust one another. We interviewed each member. In presenting the feedback, we engaged the group in action planning to deal with key issues. The group identified lack of communication as its key issue and decided to do something about it. We facilitated one-on-one communication sessions over the next month (much as described in the Application Exercise in Chapter 7's Ideas in Action). Each team member had a chance to talk about his or her working relationship with every other group member. Members revealed what they appreciated about each other and what they felt was not working. They brainstormed how to work differently. They ended their sessions by each summarizing expectations for the others and agreed on ground rules for everyone's behavior. This process and the follow-up worked for this team. Over the next year, the group progressed from being a low-trust team to being a high-trust team, and its performance excelled.

Tell the Truth

Telling the honest truth, the whole truth, is often frightening. We may wonder, will we be heard and understood? How will people react? When we lean into our fears and take a risk by telling the truth, we honor our own voice.

Although there may be a risk in being honest, there is a greater risk in being dishonest. If we speak the unvarnished truth, we may risk looking good in the eyes of our employees or our teammates. However, if we fail to tell the truth, we risk losing our credibility. We betray ourselves, and we betray the spirit of teamwork.

Effective leaders model the behavior they expect from others. If we want truth telling, we must first tell the truth. If we want our people to open up, we must first do so ourselves. We don't need to be "bleeding hearts," but we can appropriately disclose our thoughts and concerns about changes in the business environment. When we do so, it shows that we are human and do not have any hidden agendas.

The vignette at the start of this chapter illustrates what happens when team members are not forthright in their communication and are not able to tell the truth. This is a form of collusion, which is a betrayal. The underlying assumption during collusion is that team members cannot deal with openness or handle the truth. As a result, the truth goes underground.

The first step to dealing constructively with collusion is to acknowledge what is happening within the group. Once individual team members have been made aware of the dynamic, they have a responsibility to themselves and others to raise the issues. They may say to their teammates, "I think there are some issues that we have not explored openly. I would like to suggest we discuss them." For a team that has a habit of colluding, it is essential to surface the issues as they become apparent in order to break this pattern of denial. Trust has a chance to develop only when we are willing to uncover the truth and speak about it unflinchingly.

When team members do not tell the truth, they betray the very principle of teamwork. This betrayal affects all three types of transactional trust. When team members do not tell the truth, it is extremely difficult to manage expectations and follow through on agreements. When you can't count on what others say, you are reluctant to commit anything to them. Furthermore, when people are not honest, others do not trust their judgment and involve them in planning or decision making. Competence trust in one another declines. In the end, everyone loses, and team performance suffers.

Admit Mistakes

In high-trust teams, team members take responsibility for their mistakes. These teams have regular checkpoints to monitor their progress. Leaders set the tone for the team by providing safe opportunities for people to admit mistakes. They work with their employees to correct their mistakes and to learn from them.

Unfortunately, there are many teams in which this is not the case. The following observation of a supervisor in a national health-care research center describes a team climate in which admitting mistakes was not respected:

> During a team meeting, a lab technician took the initiative and admitted he made a mistake when ordering supplies for the lab. His boss at the time had a limited capacity to trust her employees and dwelled on the mistake, blaming the individual for days. The boss's behavior not only made the individual feel bad but also sent

a loud message to the other members of the lab: "It is *not* OK to make or admit mistakes."

Consequently, although team members may have been more careful in carrying out their work, they were also more cautious in taking risks of any kind. The supervisor's behavior of dwelling on the negative stifled creativity and diminished trust between her and her employees.

The type of environment just described reflects one in which people do not feel safe to admit mistakes. Errors are not viewed as learning opportunities from which value is derived. Rather, people are shamed because of the mistakes they make. The fact that the error occurred *despite one's best efforts* is overlooked. The resulting fear constrains the capacity for trust within a team. To protect themselves, team members think twice before they speak the truth and admit a mistake. In fact, they may go to great lengths to cover up mistakes to save face. The relationships within the team suffer, and trust diminishes.

Maintain Confidentiality

When team members share information in confidence, they assume it will not be shared with others. When team members have an agreement to hold certain information in confidence, they have an obligation to themselves and their teammates to uphold that agreement. If team members respect that confidence, their actions build trust. If they breach that confidence and share the information with others, trust is torn down. There is no middle ground. Their every action regarding confidential information affects trust.

This is an area where many people struggle. They want to be able to share information with others but are concerned that their confidences will not be maintained. When you are uncertain about an individual's ability to maintain information in confidence, give out only information with which you are comfortable. Breaking confidences can result in a great deal of pain and disappointment for all involved. Following is such an example.

Georgine was a member of a self-managed team of a small midwestern hospital. She was a dedicated worker but liked to talk—a lot! The team members made some ground rules regarding how they wanted to operate. One of the agreements concerned confidentiality: "What gets talked about in team meetings is team business and stays in the room." Georgine attended a skills training the hospital was sponsoring. During one of the breaks, she inadvertently shared some of the internal dynamics regarding a few of the team members. Word got back to the team via the grapevine that she was disclosing internal team business to the rest of the company. By the time the information got back, it was distorted. Team members were livid! Unfortunately, Georgine was out sick for two days after the training. Meanwhile, the story and the tension within the team escalated. When Georgine returned to work, she found out what had happened. Instead of calling the team together to discuss the facts, she was terrified and did nothing. None of her teammates brought the issue to her either. The team's trust in Georgine diminished. She was perceived as having breached the team's confidentiality. Her team members did not confront her directly and were passive-aggressive in their interactions with her. They shunned her, refusing to share with her information she needed to do her job. She was cut off socially from the group. This went on for months. The interpersonal dynamics turned sour. Morale fell, and soon so did the group's performance.

This example illustrates the pain that results from a breach of confidence. Georgine let the team and herself down. As can be expected, the team was angry and hurt. However, the other members' treatment of Georgine was as inappropriate as her breach of confidence. Rather than confront Georgine constructively, the team chose to shun her and shut her out. As trust begets trust, distrust begets distrust.

However, in the midst of betrayal there is opportunity, if we are willing to see it. "These acts of betrayal can be catalysts for change; they can actually increase trust," a sales manager pointed out. "It takes courage and the responsibility of all parties to take ownership for their roles in these circumstances."

Speak with Good Purpose

Team members wonder about the type of support they will receive from one another. They wonder how their colleagues will represent them and the team to people outside the team. They hope they will be spoken of highly and represented in a professional manner.

When team members speak with good purpose, they speak constructively and affirmatively and stand up for each other. This builds trust
within the team. Genuine support and praise for one another goes a long
way toward creating a trusting environment that produces results. "By
supporting others and receiving support in return, team members build
an interdependence based on mutual trust."[2] In addition, team members
recognize their efforts and acknowledge the contributions they make to
one another and the organization. They work harder, individually and collectively, to achieve the team's objectives and to serve their organization.

Teamwork is complex, and relationships are challenging. There are
times when team members annoy, anger, or perhaps disappoint one
another. If we contribute to these feelings in others, we hope they will
bring them directly to our attention so that we may take an active role in
resolving them. Sadly, that is not always the case.

Some people choose to voice their frustrations by gossiping and
backbiting. These are surefire ways to destroy trust in a team. These indirect tactics are done for a variety of reasons. One individual may be
uncomfortable confronting another or may feel a need to put another
down in order to raise his or her own standing. Yes, it is necessary to give
voice to our frustrations. However, we have an obligation to the relationship we have with our team members to speak directly to the individuals
involved. As one food service manager lamented, "I think people don't
want to talk to me about the issue because they feel I don't want to hear
it." If team members have things to say about an issue, they owe it to
themselves and the team to surface the issues so they can be discussed.
When team members become aware of gossip and backbiting, they have
a responsibility to stop it. Not doing so, they are contributing to the
breach of trust within their team.

COMPETENCE TRUST IN TEAMS

Respect People's Knowledge, Skills, and Abilities

People generally enter teams wanting to make a contribution. However,
they may be concerned about their ability to do so. They may wonder,
"Will I be able to learn the new skills required of me so that I do not let
my team or my boss down?" These are very real concerns and can cause

much anxiety. Especially since fear begets fear and self-distrust begets self-distrust, they feed on each other. Left unchecked, they can materialize into a self-fulfilling reality. The very thing we fear, we create or bring upon ourselves. When we focus on our fear, we lose sight of our trust in ourselves. We betray ourselves.

Team members can do a great deal to help one another deal with these anxieties. With ever-increasing marketplace demands and technological advancements, it is not unusual for a team's work to require a skill set or knowledge base that does not currently exist within the team. However, a leader or team members may recognize the capability of one of their own to acquire it. When others see you as competent and they trust in your basic ability, their trust can help you trust in your own ability to learn new skills.

When people feel their competence is trusted and their work is appreciated, they can get excited about what they are doing and with whom they are doing it. They feel able to take risks and explore new arenas. "The opportunity to make a difference does that to people: it keeps them coming back for more."[3]

Bert was scared to death. His stomach was in knots, his palms were sweating, and his breathing was pacing fast. He had never given a public presentation, and in thirty minutes he would be speaking to sixty-five managers on behalf of his team. He did not want to let the other members down. The team had been working on this project for six months, and this presentation was key to getting approval on the project.

The team leader, Jo Anne, offered reassurance. "You are respected by the managers of this organization, and I know you will do a wonderful job. Relax and enjoy yourself." Well, Bert did not relax until he was halfway through his presentation, and he did not enjoy himself until it was over, but he did a wonderful job, and the presentation was well received. The team won the approval!

Bert's team members saw an ability he had to connect with people and earn their respect, a gift he was not aware of himself. The trust his team members had in him enabled him to step into his discomfort zone.

It provided him with an opportunity to develop new abilities and discover new ways of seeing himself.

Unfortunately, team members' skills and abilities are not always trusted. In these situations, rather than feeling acknowledged and respected, people feel discounted. As one concerned employee lamented to a teammate, "I feel discounted. My knowledge is perceived as a threat to you. Yet I want to be a resource to you."

There are times when team members do not see one another as the whole people that they are. Their narrow perceptions limit the potential of their teammates, as individuals and the team, as a whole. When team members feel discounted or experience other members being discounted, it is necessary to communicate your concerns. When people discount one another, their comments reflect more about them than the person they are attacking. Their comments are often the result of their own insecurity, fear, lack of information, or need to control.

Ned makes his presence known. At team meetings, he dominates the discussions. If any of the other team members try to offer their perspectives, he verbally attacks them. No matter what the topic, he has an opinion, and he is always "right." The rest of the team acquiesces to him. He bullies the others, and they give him power. They are afraid of him. Team members have difficulty saying exactly what is on their minds because of him. They need to learn how to handle him. The rest of the team needs to stop him, call his bluff, and speak up. The others should refuse to give him any more power. It takes a bit of courage, but it will help this team tremendously.

In such team situations, it is important to facilitate an open dialogue among team members to clear the air. If members consistently feel discounted, they need to feel safe enough to express their frustrations and vent their concerns without being further discounted. The bully needs to be confronted head-on; consequences for his behavior need to be spelled out unequivocally, and discipline needs to be enforced. When team members are encouraged, they will start speaking up, taking a stand. As they experience some success, their confidence and competence in handling these situations grow, thereby freeing up their energy for more productive purposes.

Involve Others and Seek Their Input

In high-trust teams, members involve one another and seek their input in the team's day-to-day work. They share information, exchange ideas, brainstorm solutions. By actively involving one another in their processes, they support one another's goals and contribute to the total performance of the team. This support builds confidence and competence trust within each individual and the team as a whole.

In low-trust teams, members do not readily involve others or seek their input on decisions. People operate in "silos," and there is not much collaboration or interdependence. One indication of a low-trust team is the "not invented here" syndrome. When this syndrome is present, people do not respect each other's ideas. Team members will ignore or discount others' ideas or other teams' suggestions simply because they didn't think of them first. Not valuing the input of others' work, team members do not benefit from the collective learning that could take place. They do not gain from each other's competence, and the performance of the team and the overall organization suffers.

Furthermore, when leaders don't value the contributions of their team members, they discount their employees and discredit themselves.

The manager asked the team to develop procedures for inspecting parts on the production line. Rallying to his request, the team worked hard for almost five weeks to develop the procedures. The team felt proud of what it had accomplished. At the end of the five weeks, the supervisor ignored the team's work and instituted his own procedures without any explanation to his team. Team members became discouraged and felt resigned: "Why should we work to give him what he asks for? He'll simply ignore it anyway!"

The supervisor initially sought the input of his team, yet his actions did not respect the members' work or the value of their contribution. He demonstrated poor judgment and a lack of competence trust in them. Giving people an opportunity to contribute, whetting their appetites and firing their enthusiasm and then dashing their spirits, dishonors the relationship. It wastes your people's time and energy and destroys their trust in you as their leader.

Help People Learn Skills

When team members don't feel acknowledged for the skills, knowledge, and experience they bring to the organization, they stop giving their utmost to that organization. They may go through the motions, but internally they shut down and resign themselves to giving as little as possible.

After a prolonged time, when members don't feel valued for the capabilities they bring to the team, they begin to question their own competence. Their willingness to learn and take risks falters. Their capacity for trust in themselves decreases.

To retain talented employees, effective leaders know that they need to acknowledge their employees' contributions and challenge these individuals' capabilities to grow. To build the capacity of their people, leaders need to push their employees out of their comfort zones. The most powerful learning takes place just outside an individual's comfort zone. Yet leaders need to support their employees in their discomfort. They make the discomfort acceptable. By supporting employees through their discomfort, they help the employees increase their capacity to learn and to trust in themselves.

There are numerous ways to help team members develop their capacity and strengthen their competence trust in one another. One method is for team members to share their skills with each other: "Each one teach one" (recall Application Exercise A in Chapter 8's Ideas in Action). This is an opportunity for team members to articulate the skills they have and the ones they want to learn. Have team members contract with one another for the skills they want to learn from the person who possesses that knowledge. If the skill set exists outside the team, have members contract with the appropriate resources. After learning the skills, it is their responsibility to bring their learning back to the team and teach a teammate. Teaching one another helps reinforce learning, builds competence trust in one another, and develops the capacity of the team.

Practicing the behaviors of each of the three types of transactional trust builds trust in teams. In developing contractual trust, teams are best served when they manage expectations, honor agreements, and encourage mutually serving intentions. In growing communication trust, teams work well when they share information, admit mistakes, maintain confidentiality, and speak with good purpose. In fostering competence trust, teams develop when they respect people's knowledge, skills, and abilities, involve others and seek their input, and help people learn new skills. Building and maintaining trust in teams requires constant attention to these behaviors.

IDEAS IN ACTION

Here we present questions and exercises leaders can use to rebuild trust within their teams.

Questions to Consider

Reflect privately on the following questions, and record your thoughts. If you are working with a team, have team members share their thoughts with one another. Discuss issues and record next steps.

1. Think of a team in which the trust among team members was high. How did that high level of trust affect the effectiveness of the team? In what ways were members more productive due to the high level of trust?

2. Think of a team where trust was low, perhaps as a result of having experienced betrayal. What was the impact of this low trust on the team's effectiveness? How did the low trust reduce the team's productivity?

3. Did members of the low-trust team have explicit agreements? Were they upheld? Were there areas where the team needed agreements but was unable to negotiate or commit to them?

4. How was the high-trust team able to share information? How did that sharing of information contribute to the team's effectiveness? What happened to team members when they made a mistake, whether they admitted it or not?

5. Was the competence of members of the low-trust team identified and systematically used? What was the effect on team cooperation

when competence was either not recognized or not used? Was any attention given to improving the capabilities of team members?

Application Exercises

The following exercises are intended to facilitate building trust within a group or team.

A. *Conduct Dialogue Sessions.* The Reina Trust & Betrayal Model can serve as a framework for opening up dialogue about the critical trust-related issues in a team. It is useful for helping teams heighten their level of awareness regarding what trust means to each team member, develop a common language to discuss trust-related issues, and develop trust-building skills and practices they could implement to take action on trust-related issues in their respective departments.

The model is constructed in such a way that you can use the figures individually or sequentially as part of a whole process. Following are suggestions of how to apply the model when working with teams.

1. Start by asking participants what their definition of trust is. Have people reflect on, record, and share their definitions with the group.
2. Referring to Figures 5A, 5B, and 5C (Transactional Trust), review the three different types of transactional trust and the behaviors under each type.
3. Ask the group what behaviors contribute to fostering an environment of trust within your organization and which hinder or destroy trust within the organization.

After reviewing the Transactional Trust figures refer to Figure 1 (Capacity for Trust), Figure 2 (Capacity for Trust Scales), Figure 3 (Betrayal) and Figure 4 (Seven Steps for Healing from Betrayal) for guidance in understanding the differences in each person's capacity for trust and the steps needed for teams to heal from betrayal.

B. *Coach Your Employees and Mediate Conflict.* The Reina Trust & Betrayal Model is also useful for coaching employees to higher performance. In one-on-one sessions, a manager and an employee can jointly look at the trust-building behaviors in which the individual is strong and discuss those that the employee needs to develop to increase his or her leadership capabilities. The model can also be employed as a tool in mediating conflict between two individuals. It provides a visual guide to help shift the conflicting individuals from blaming each other toward more objectively looking at the issues and what actions need to be taken to alleviate those issues.

Instructions:

Whether you wish to coach an employee to higher performance or mediate a conflict between two individuals;

1. Turn to Figures 5A, 5B, and 5C of the Reina Trust & Betrayal Model. Review the behaviors within each form of Transitional Trust with the individuals.

2. In coaching individual performance: What are the behaviors within each type of trust that are this person's strengths? Which are areas for improvement?

3. In mediating conflict between individuals: What behaviors within each type of trust have contributed to the conflict? What behaviors within each type of trust need to be addressed to resolve the dispute?

C. *Develop the Team's Capacity for Trust.* Use our adaptation of the fishbone diagram on the next page to analyze the trust-building behaviors that support the development of the team's capacity to trust. (This framework may also be used to identify the behaviors that destroy trust within the team.) Suggested steps are as follows:

1. Draw a circle on the right side of a piece of flipchart paper and label it "Team's Capacity for Trust." Then draw three branches extending from the left side of the circle, and label each with one of the three types of transactional trust: "Contractual Trust," "Communication Trust," and "Competence Trust," as in the figure.

2. Have the team identify the specific behaviors that foster development of the team's capacity to trust. Record them on the branches under each of the respective types of trust (for example, "Establish working agreements" under "Contractual Trust," "Share more information" under "Communication Trust").

3. Analyze the behaviors that are the weakest under each type of trust. Discuss ways to strengthen these behaviors.

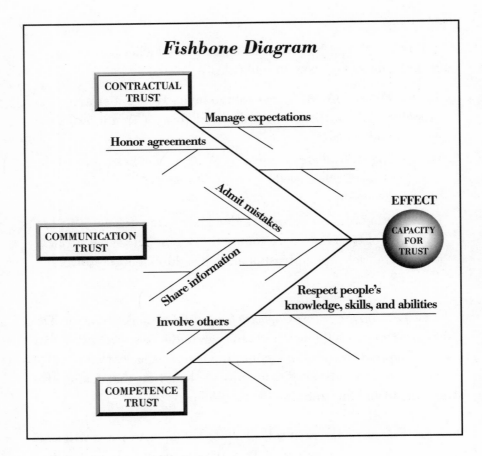

Fishbone Diagram

10

REBUILDING TRUST
IN ORGANIZATIONS

Trust is the lubricant for individual and organizational change.
JAMES M. KOUZES AND BARRY Z. POSNER

In this chapter, you will learn about:

- The impact of change on people
- When people see change as loss
- Dealing with the emotional side of change
- Applying the Reina Trust & Betrayal Model to help people heal from betrayal

It was a Tuesday in November, cold, damp, and overcast, as many are in the North. At the plant, anxiety was high and morale was low. In the lunchroom, people speculated about what was to come next. "Have you heard when the next cut will be? Who do you think will go this time?" A worker from across the table chimed in, "I have given seventeen years of faithful service to this company. From now on, I don't trust anybody—it's every man for himself!" Out on the production line, employees were moving the product, but performance was nothing like a year earlier, before the restructuring began. The plant manager peered out of his upper mezzanine office window overlooking the production floor. *"Overall labor costs are lower, production is down and declining, and morale has hit rock bottom!"* he muttered to himself. *"What am I going to do?"*

Stories like this are commonplace. Change is happening in all organizations—it is essential if they don't want to be left behind. Leaders face the challenge of managing change in a way that is the least damaging to trust. They cannot afford the repercussions of destroyed trust.

Traditionally, leaders have approached change from the perspective of "what is good for the organization is good for employees." Yet many of these change efforts have failed to produce the desired results. Not wanting to repeat the same mistakes, conscientious leaders today are aware that the decisions they make for the good of the organization also affect people's lives. Savvy leaders recognize that they still have to make the tough decisions, but they understand that how they implement those decisions influences their employee's trust and commitment. Consequently, they feel a responsibility to manage the change with dignity and respect for all involved. They know that hanging on to talented employees affects their competitive edge and the bottom line. They also know that successful change efforts build trust with their people before, during, and after major change initiatives.

THE IMPACT OF CHANGE ON PEOPLE

Organizations depend on relationships to get most work done and to coordinate the efforts of their workforces. Relationships depend on trust to succeed. When leaders lose sight of this and orchestrate change without sensitivity and awareness toward the people affected by the change, they betray themselves and the people both. Let us look at two examples of ways in which the mechanics of managing change overshadowed the human element and compromised people's dignity and respect.

Helen was conducting an outplacement seminar designed to offer support to people who had just lost their jobs. Ten minutes before the session was to begin, Helen stepped into the hallway for some water when a manager approached her. "Helen," he asked, "can you hold up the session for fifteen minutes? I have two employees who need to be in your workshop today but haven't been informed yet!" The manager wanted to include in the session two employees who were getting laid off, but he had not yet told them they were losing their jobs.

The manager in this vignette was insensitive to the needs of his employees. He was going to rush into informing them that they were losing their jobs and then send them immediately into a workshop about outplacement. Following is another anecdote illustrating insensitivity to the needs of people in managing change.

Over a number of months, as the XYZ Company downsized one of their divisions, they sold unneeded hardware and furniture. Following an employee's last day, the furniture was removed from their office. Ian, a purchasing agent within this division, knew he was going to go through some type of job transition but did not know when it would happen or what it would be like. He was hoping for a transfer to another branch of the company. One Monday Ian came into work and discovered that his desk and chair were gone. When he inquired about the missing furniture, he learned that he was out of a job.

Organizational change doesn't have to happen as in these examples. The betrayal people experience is not necessarily a result of downsizing or major change but as a result of how it is managed. Employees want to be a part of the process, not apart from the process, and they need time and assistance to adjust to the changes. All employees, leaving and staying, deserve to be treated with trust, dignity, and respect. How leaders manage change within their organizations affects their employees' trust and morale and the desired outcomes of the changes themselves.

WHEN PEOPLE SEE CHANGE AS LOSS

People may experience any change as a loss—the loss of fellow workers being laid off, the guilt of good performers losing their jobs, or the dissolution of the "family" company environment that once existed. People may resent the fact that they are doing much more work for the same pay and that opportunities to earn more are limited or nonexistent.

With every change comes both gain and loss. In organizations, often one person's gain is another person's loss. People making the changes are usually the ones to gain. If I am the one gaining, it is harder for me to see how the other person loses. Culturally, we are taught that it is not good to cause other people to lose, so we mentally minimize their loss. This phenomenon makes it harder for us see the pain many employees experience with change.

Often the organization in which people work is not the same place they "signed on for" initially. People may experience major changes as losses. They need to talk about and grieve for those losses. The longer the employee's tenure, the greater the feelings of loss and the greater the need to grieve. And in a world where everything is changing rapidly, many people who previously looked to their workplace as a source of stability now regard it as out of control. It frightens them.

DEALING WITH THE EMOTIONAL SIDE OF CHANGE

Dealing with the emotional side of change is difficult but necessary. Many leaders are uncomfortable watching their people experience the pain of change and are uncomfortable experiencing their own pain. They often consider this to be "touchy-feely" stuff, not the stuff of "real business." During times of change, leaders tend to retreat to the "hard side" of business for many reasons. It is where they are most comfortable, where their role is more tangibly defined, where they are skilled, and where they are the safest. In the retreat to the safe side, they fail to honor themselves, their relationships, and the real needs of the people they serve. They fail to honor the essence of leadership. Their search for safety results in a betrayal of themselves and others.

Effective leaders understand what betrayal does to themselves, to others, and to the organizational system. They recognize the high cost of betrayal. It robs individuals of their ability to believe in themselves.

Their capacity to trust contracts, and this ultimately diminishes their ability to contribute wholeheartedly to the organization. When people feel betrayed, they are not motivated to perform. Employees reciprocate by doing enough to get by but not enough to make the changes succeed. Within a short time, productivity is adversely affected. "When people react negatively to change—such as downsizing—it shows up in reduced productivity and low morale. The real cause is that people's self-esteem is threatened."[1]

Effective leaders acknowledge their employees' feelings of fear and loss and work to restore their confidence. Otherwise, the betrayal continues, and people's capacity to trust in their leaders and their organization diminishes. Survivors go into a state of resignation: they take fewer risks, blame others, and are not as productive as they once were. If employees have been burnt before, they are less willing to give their all and come through when needed. If leaders do not deal with feelings of betrayal, they will unwittingly destroy two of the very qualities they need to be competitive: their employees' trust and their performance.

HELPING PEOPLE HEAL FROM BETRAYAL

We have explored the variety of ways in which people experience betrayal. In organizations, quite often, betrayal is experienced when changes occur. The Reina Trust & Betrayal Model provides a framework to honor relationships while managing change. Here we explore how the Seven Steps for Healing from Betrayal (see Figure 4 in Chapter 5) can help you overcome betrayal in your organization and manage the change process.

When helping organizations deal with betrayal, we must acknowledge that people, individually and collectively, feel betrayed and then help them recover. As a leader, certain acts that you do now can have a positive impact on people, just as previous acts resulted in feelings of betrayal. Our model is designed to help you remain aware of the behaviors essential to healing that are too easily dropped, especially during times of rapid change. Our model also provides a common language and perspective that may be shared to foster greater understanding and healing with people, individually and collectively.

Step 1: Observe and Acknowledge What Has Happened

Start with awareness.   Similar to healing at the individual level, the first step to healing at the organizational level requires awareness. One of the greatest mistakes leaders can make in challenging times is to assume that once a major change such as a downsizing, restructuring, merger, or other "traumatic workplace event" has taken place, trust will return on its own. This view is both unrealistic and irresponsible. Effective leaders acknowledge the negative impact change has on their employees' morale and productivity. They realize that employees come to work as full human beings with feelings. They know that people who do not have a supportive environment to deal with their feelings and concerns constructively are much less able to heal from their experience of betrayal.

Assess the health of your organization.   Observe and assess the climate within the organization. Notice what your people are experiencing and acknowledge it. Find out what is important to them. Listen to what they are saying at the water cooler, in the break rooms, and on the shop floor. When witnessing anger, don't just notice the anger but look past it to see whether the person is expressing hurt and disappointment too. Quite often people express deeper feelings of hurt and disappointment through anger. Remember, people in pain need to be listened to. They need someone they can trust to turn to for support and understanding.

Acknowledge feelings.   To start the healing process, effective leaders consciously acknowledge their employees' feelings of betrayal. It is only after acknowledging the feelings of betrayal that they are able to respond to them. Leaders must work very hard to not get defensive or try to justify or rationalize what happened. They must remember that people are entitled to their feelings. It is the role of a leader to listen, observe, and acknowledge. This is the first step to healing the wounds.

Step 2: Allow Employees' Feelings to Surface

Give people permission.   Give employees permission to externalize their feelings, in a constructive manner. Create safe forums staffed

by skilled facilitators that support the expression of fear, anger, and frustrations regarding organizational changes. Giving your employees a constructive way to discuss their feelings and experiences helps them let go
of the negativity they are holding, freeing up that energy for rebuilding
relationships and returning their focus to performance.

Help people verbalize.   Help employees give voice to their
pain—pain they are afraid or unable to share with anyone. When you give
your attention to understanding your employees, you let them know that
you respect their pain.

This is the difficult work for leaders. But it is important and necessary work in facilitating healing from betrayal. Your employees don't care
how much you know until they know how much you care—about them
and their well-being. People in pain need to have their feelings heard.
They need to know that you are able to relate to what they are saying and
feeling. When you do not acknowledge your employees' emotions, they
feel unheard, resentful, and distrusting toward you. Another layer of
betrayal occurs.

Step 3: Give Employees Support

Recognize your employees' transitional needs.   People have
transitional needs that must be met before they can adapt to change.
They have informational needs regarding the new direction the organization is taking and the strategies it proposes to get there. They have relationship needs associated with belonging and their role in the new
organization. And they have personal needs such as feeling valued. When
leaders expect people to embrace change without these fundamental
needs' being met, people feel betrayed.

Leaders can avoid creating feelings of betrayal by drawing on the
behaviors of transaction trust. First, they realize that although you may
be orchestrating the transition, you know that each employee has to do
the work for which he or she is responsible. Each employee has to take
the initiative and make the commitment to make adjustments to be a contributing member in the new work environment. Leaders can foster contractual trust by clearly stating their expectations of people. Let people

know explicitly what you are looking for from them and what they may expect from you in return. If you sense that they may have expectations of you that you are not able to fulfill, tell the truth, let them know you are not able to deliver on those expectations and why. It is appropriate to emphasize the importance of continuous improvement and changing job roles as a vehicle to further the development of people's competence. You may help ease anxieties people may associate with these expectations by demonstrating your trust in their competence.

Second, emphasize to employees the importance of building new relationships, internally and externally. Share with them your desire to build your relationship with them on a foundation of trust. You may encourage them to develop working agreements to foster the development of trust. Third, conduct discussions with employees to build communication trust. This is an opportunity to share information, to clarify priorities, and to help people understand how the organizational change affects work responsibilities and expectations. This is also an opportunity for you to ask for and receive feedback regarding how people are feeling about what is happening and how it is happening. Your actions during discussions demonstrate that it is safe for people to let you know honestly how they feel about what they are hearing. Let them see that it is OK to ask questions and challenge assumptions.

Back your employees.   Your leadership position allows you to be your employees' advocate. Therefore, represent your people's interests, defend them from unwarranted criticism, and lobby for resources critical to their job. By backing your people, you are building contractual trust and meeting the implicit expectations people have of leaders. Furthermore, you demonstrate that you can be trusted to fulfill future commitments, that your people can count on you to do what you say you will do.

Being perceived as their greatest support becomes a basis for rebuilding trust when two preconditions are satisfied. First, it must be deserved support—their requests must be justifiable. Second, it must be sincere. Your support must come from an authentic desire to do what is right, fair, and good. It cannot be an attempt to manipulate people's perceptions.[2] When it comes from who you really are, it is received as authentic and is therefore reciprocated.

Step 4: Reframe the Experience

Put the experience into a larger context. Helping your employees work through their emotions makes it possible for them to begin to put their betrayal behind them. This distance provides you with an opportunity to rebuild communication trust by discussing the bigger picture, the business reasons for change. Honestly acknowledge the changes the company went through and why. In doing so, it is critical to acknowledge what people have experienced. Only then will employees be in a position to listen to and understand the new direction in which the organization is headed and to see their role in it.

The process of healing from betrayal is an inquiry. The questions that people ask will guide the journey.[3] Answering their questions honestly will provide employees with understanding, awareness, truth, and renewed hope for a trusting relationship with you and the organization.

Help them realize there are choices. Experiencing betrayal leaves employees feeling very vulnerable and at the mercy of the forces of change. They will need help seeing that they have choices regarding how they react to their circumstances. The more people are aware that they can choose their actions, the more they are able to take responsibility for those actions. Employees will need help checking out their assumptions, breaking out of their self-limiting beliefs, and exploring options and possibilities.

Embrace failure. Some of the behaviors we have been discussing that aid in healing from betrayal may be new for you. They may be behaviors in which you are not as trusting of your competence. Therefore, it may take some practice developing these skills and becoming comfortable using them. During this time, you may make some mistakes. That does not automatically make you a failure. You must embrace your mistakes as opportunities for learning, thereby turning them to your own benefit. After all, they provide valuable feedback regarding what works and what does not.

Just as leaders must be sensitive to employees' needs, employees need to be sensitive to leaders' needs. This may mean having some patience and understanding that the leader is grappling with change as well. Therefore, if a leader makes a mistake, that is not necessarily evidence that the leader can't be trusted. It is evidence that the leader is stretching, growing, and learning. While you are practicing new ways of relating, people need to be supportive and understanding of your learning.

To gain support and understanding, it may be helpful to share with people that you are learning new skills. Sharing this aspect of yourself demonstrates your trust in them and further extends the invitation to rebuild your relationship with them.

Step 5: Take Responsibility

Take responsibility for your role in the process. It is not helpful to try to cover up mistakes. It does not serve you or the relationship. Something quite powerful occurs when we tell the impeccable truth—with no exceptions, no justifications, no rationalizations. Telling the truth is the fundamental basis for trust in workplace relationships. It demonstrates one's trustworthiness.

Make amends, and return with dividends. It is the leader's role to break the chain of betrayal and reverse the spiral of distrust. Since actions speak louder than words, it is important that you take the first step in mending fences with your employees. Remember that rebuilding trust does not simply mean giving back what was taken away. It means returning something in better shape than it was originally in. If you have lost trust by taking valued responsibilities away, you can regain trust by granting people even more significant responsibilities.[4] You must not only replace but make things better. If this is not possible, be honest about the realities of the situation and what you can do to make amends.

Manage expectations. The level of expectations is directly correlated to the opportunity for betrayal. To safeguard yourself and your employees against future betrayals, keenly manage expectations. Employees want to know honestly what is expected of them and what they can expect in return. Emphasize the need to negotiate expectations when you feel they cannot be fulfilled. This strengthens contractual trust between you and your employees.

Keep your promises. Managing promises is important in managing relationships. Trust is the result of promises kept. Don't make promises you know you can't keep; that just sets you and everyone with whom you have a relationship up for a downfall. When you realize that you cannot keep promises, renegotiate them; don't break them.

Be careful of what you promise and what you *appear* to promise. When you are attempting to rebuild trust, it is essential that you not try to justify past actions and that you address the perceptions of those who feel betrayed. "It is enough for an employee to have *believed* that a promise was broken for trust to be violated."[5]

Step 6: Forgive

Shift from blaming to focusing on needs.   Persistent resentment and blame in an organization are toxic to the individuals involved and to the whole system. They undermine trust, morale, productivity, creativity, and innovation. People continue to blame when they perceive that those who are responsible have failed to take responsibility. They in return feel that they do not have to take action and are therefore not responsible.

Since forgiveness is a personal matter, it is difficult for people to forgive a system. However, leaders can begin to cultivate a more personal and trusting climate where healing and forgiveness can take place. They can begin to do this by helping people shift from blaming the organization or its leaders to helping them focus on their personal needs.

It is essential that leaders help people shift from a blaming mode to problem-solving focus. What do your employees need to resolve the issues, concerns, fears, and pain they are feeling? What conversations need to take place? What still needs to be said? What needs to happen for healing to occur? What will make the difference, right now?

Recognize that forgiveness is freedom.   Forgiveness is about freeing ourselves and others from the burdens of the past. When we help people forgive others, we help them free themselves. With forgiveness, they heal for their future by changing their attitude about the past. We help them see new possibilities.

For most people, forgiveness takes time, and it happens a little at a time. However, having some understanding of the circumstances surrounding the betrayal helps make forgiveness easier. Over time, your employees may be willing to forgive, but they will not necessarily forget. You can help them heal from the pain they felt, but you cannot erase the events of the past. Occasionally, your employees may still be a bit angry after they forgive. It is natural that they may experience lingering feelings of anger for the perceived wrongs they experienced.

Step 7: Let Go and Move On

Accept what's so.   Leaders can help their people accept what has happened. Acceptance is not condoning what was done but experiencing the reality of what happened without denying, disowning, or resenting it. It is facing the truth without blame. It is helping employees separate themselves from their preoccupation with the past and helping them invest their emotional energies in the present and in creating a different future.

Realize that you won't always win.   Although you may not always win, it is important that you make a good-faith effort and that your intentions are honorable. It is quite acceptable for leaders to disagree with their employees or not support a particular cause. Effective leaders do so with honesty and integrity.

Take the time, make the commitment.   Building trust takes time and commitment. When trust is lost, it is regained only by a sincere dedication to the key behaviors and practices that earned it in the first place. The road back is not easy. However, by listening, telling the truth, keeping your promises, and backing your employees, you will play an instrumental role in assisting your employees and organization to heal from betrayal and rebuild trust.

Let us end with some wise words from James Kouzes and Barry Pozner: "Before people will be willing to follow a leader's vision or act on a leader's initiatives, they must trust their leader. This trust cannot be demanded. Leaders must earn it."[6]

IDEAS IN ACTION

Here we present questions and exercises leaders can use to facilitate rebuilding trust in their organizations.

Questions to Consider

Reflect privately on the following questions, and record your thoughts. If you are working with a team, have team members share their thoughts with each other.

1. Think of a major organizational change that reduced the trust within an organization or even caused a sense of betrayal. What did leaders do that contributed to the betrayal?
2. In this betrayal situation, in what ways did leaders acknowledge, if at all, the emotional price paid by employees? How did the emotional side of this change affect productivity within the organization?
3. After the betrayal occurred, what steps, if any, did the leadership take to promote healing from the betrayal? What would you recommend leaders do to help themselves and their employees let go of the past and move forward?
4. During a major organizational change, what would you recommend leaders do to address the needs of employees? What would you recommend for managing the new expectations that are being created during this change process?
5. How could leaders reframe change in terms of a larger context that would make sense to employees?

Application Exercises

The following exercises are intended to facilitate the development of trust within your organization.

A. *Cultivating Trust in Your Organization: The Role of the Senior Management Team.* Senior management teams need to look at the issue of trust within their organization systemically. Collectively, they address the question, "How do we, as a senior management team, cultivate trust within our organization?" In doing so, they explore ways in which they can provide overarching structure and resources to support the work of the frontline managers and employees.

Instructions:

1. Allocate an uninterrupted block of time for the senior management team to explore the following systemic questions as they relate to your organization. (Offsite retreat settings are ideal for this kind of work.)

- What does a culture of trust look like within our organization?
- What and where are our critical trust-related issues?
- What are the biggest barriers to cultivating trust in our organization?

- What policies and procedures are detrimental to trust between departments and across the organization?
- What policies and procedures do we need to rethink, rework, or rewrite?
- What does each senior manager need in his or her respective division to support the people in the field serving customers?
- What are the three top needs in each department? What can the members of the senior management team collectively do to support each other in meeting those needs?

2. Designate a skilled facilitator to lead the discussion making sure roles and working agreements are in place.
3. Capture key points regarding each question on a flipchart. Identify essential issues to work on.
4. Prioritize the top three issues and create an action plan to address them.

Addressing these questions collectively not only begins the process of building trust within the organizational system but also starts the process of building trust among individuals within the senior management team.

B. *Identifying Behaviors That Create or Destroy Trust.* A senior management team (or any team) may use a "force field analysis" like that shown on page 149 to identify which behaviors support or create trust and which behaviors detract from and destroy trust within the organization. Suggested steps are as follows:

1. Draw a large T on a piece of flipchart paper, and label the top center "Trust Within Our Organization." Then label the left and right columns "Create Trust" and "Destroy Trust," respectively. (Other possible headings are "Help" and "Hinder" or "Driving Forces" and "Restraining Forces.")
2. Have the team identify the specific behaviors that create and destroy trust within the organization and list them in the appropriate column.
3. Rank and prioritize the behaviors under each column. Select the three behaviors that destroy the most.
4. Strategize ways to resolve these three troublesome behaviors.

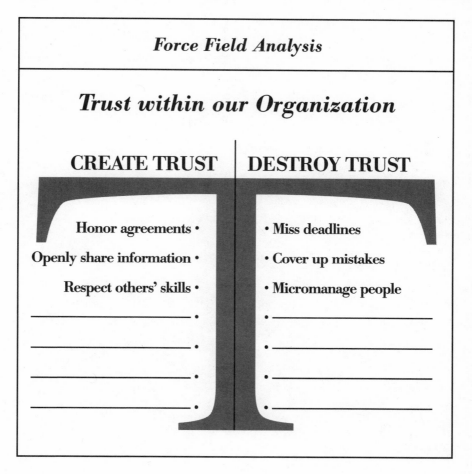

Force Field Analysis

Trust within our Organization

CREATE TRUST	DESTROY TRUST
Honor agreements •	• Miss deadlines
Openly share information •	• Cover up mistakes
Respect others' skills •	• Micromanage people
_____ •	• _____
_____ •	• _____
_____ •	• _____
_____ •	• _____

TRANSFORMATIVE TRUST

Transforming organizations to become more trusting and productive environments is the challenge of leaders today and the work of leaders tomorrow. In Part III, we explore what Transformative Trust is and what it takes to create it and nurture it in your organization.

11

TRANSFORMATIVE TRUST

Trust is the final stage in humankind's
evolutionary process toward wholeness.
PAUL BRENNER

In this chapter, you will learn about:

- A definition of Transformative Trust
- The nature of Transformative Trust
- The four core characteristics of Transformative Trust

Faced with a strategic business decision handed down from corporate headquarters, the "Jones Company," a division of a Fortune 100 company, had to lay off 100 people from its 420-person operation in a one-company town in rural America. It was a decision in which local leadership was not involved. It was the first time ever, since the division started up ten years prior, that there had been this type of change.

Although the local managers were not involved in the initial decision to reduce the division's workforce, they were fully responsible for implementing the change. They were committed to doing so in a way that honored their people and all that the departing employees had offered the organization. They carefully orchestrated each phase of the process.

These leaders were sensitive to their employees' needs and acknowledged the impact of this change. "We know this is affecting your lives dramatically," the division manager said, holding back tears. To ensure that people remained fully informed, top management set up open lines of communication, held special meetings and forums to inform people every step of the way, and made sure everyone heard the same message at the same time, in person. Through the process, the leaders were visible, accessible, and approachable. They went onto the shop floor to listen to the concerns of their employees firsthand. Leaders were available around the clock, all three shifts, to talk to their people, answer their questions, listen to their concerns, and inform them of the next steps as they developed. The leaders made sure that all concerns raised were acknowledged and addressed, even if it took some time and research.

Management worked diligently to assist the affected employees. The managers set up career counseling and outplacement centers, visited with management in other organizations to explore job opportunities for those leaving, and invited companies into the plant to meet with job candidates. Within five months, all of the displaced employees who wanted to continue to work had been placed in new jobs, inside or outside the corporation.

Throughout the process, everyone in the organization was kept aware of all activities associated with the changes. Managers and human resource personnel facilitated focus group discussions for the survivors throughout the company to allow employees to voice their concerns and frustrations.

Throughout this traumatic time, trust was cultivated by the behaviors of this organization's leaders. Their conviction to honor their role as leaders, their courage to tell the "hard" truth at all times, their compassion to remain sensitive to the impact of the change on people's lives, and their awareness of community made a difference. Leaders were able to cultivate trust in an adverse situation because they cared about the people in their organization and how those people were affected by this experience.

A DEFINITION OF TRANSFORMATIVE TRUST

Transformative trust occurs when the amount of trust within a team or organization reaches a critical point and increases exponentially, becoming self-generating and synergistic. Four core characteristics are usually present: conviction, courage, compassion, and community.

THE NATURE OF TRANSFORMATIVE TRUST

As we have discussed, trust starts as a transaction. "You have to give it to get it." Yet when relationships are honored and the behaviors of transactional trust are consciously practiced, the level of trust reaches a critical point. It experiences a multiplier effect whereby we receive more than we originally gave. Every time trust is offered, greater trust is returned. Trust between people takes on a dynamic energy and force of its own. People feel good about their relationships and are excited about their work and their colleagues on the job. They feel believed in and therefore believe in what they are doing. They feel acknowledged and respected. As a result, they show up for work alert and excited, knowing that what they do makes a difference.

In work environments where transformative trust unfolds, individuals learn to work constructively with their need for power and control. They learn to manage their assumptions and fears and their need to protect their positions and expertise. The capacity to trust in relationships between individuals, among teams, and across the organization expands.

Just as betrayal decreases our capacity for trust by striking at the very core of our being in a painful way, transformative trust increases our capacity for trust by speaking to that same core of our humanness in a nurturing way. Betrayal and distrust come from a place of deprivation or scarcity, whereas transformative trust comes from a place of abundance.

Transformative trust in organizations is the hope and vision of the future. It is the work of today's leaders to raise the level of consciousness and awareness among themselves and their people regarding behaviors that develop trust and those that destroy it. In doing so, workplace relationships may receive what they truly deserve: to be honored, respected, and nurtured.

This is not easy work. Together we are partners in the process of learning and discovering more about this complex dynamic. In this chapter, we explore what this means to leaders and employees alike every day on the job. We will further explore how leaders can bring themselves to their work and make a difference.

THE FOUR CORE CHARACTERISTICS OF TRANSFORMATIVE TRUST

As a colleague pointed out, "Building trust is more than just showing up. It is showing up as a total, whole self." The role of leadership provides you with an opportunity to create transformative trust in your organizations. It cannot be mandated; it must be invited. It is not created instantly; it takes time to develop and mature. In the high-pressure world of most organizations, creating transformative trust requires leaders to demonstrate and support the four core characteristics of transformative trust: conviction, courage, compassion, and community (see Figure 6).

It takes conviction, courage, compassion, and community to move individuals, teams, or organizations out of betrayal and toward a trusting workplace environment. It takes conviction to acknowledge the truth about dynamics people have experienced. It takes courage to honor relationships when the going gets tough and we are truly challenged. It takes compassion to forgive ourselves and others for mistakes and transgressions. It takes a sense of community to reframe painful situations and take responsibility to help people understand what they have experienced, draw on it in constructive ways, let go, and move on.

It takes the four C's of transformative trust to practice the behaviors of transactional trust (contractual, communication, and competence trust) day in and day out. When we trust in ourselves, listen to our hearts, and act out of the goodness of our souls, we are being true to ourselves. When we speak and act with conviction, courage, compassion, and community, we help others heal, and we help ourselves heal. What results is powerful! Transactional trust, working with the four C's, increases people's capacity for trust and transforms the quality of relationships.

Conviction

The strength of our convictions starts with self-awareness. Becoming aware of what is really meaningful is critical to self-awareness and the development of one's capacity for trust. What are the things you will "go to the wall" for? That is where your passion resides. When we are true to ourselves and have passion and conviction in what we believe, people concur in what we are saying and trust us. They trust that we are guided by our convictions and are committed to making those convictions happen. Being clear in our convictions builds trust with others and strengthens our capacity for trust in ourselves. Trust in oneself is the greatest asset a leader can have, especially in times of change. Yet when we stray from those convictions, those personal truths, we betray ourselves and others.

It is ironic how many times we trust the instincts of others before our own. How often we betray ourselves! And what are the consequences of doing so? When we don't listen to our own voice, trust our instincts, and live by our convictions, we break our spirits and diminish our capacity for trust.

The people we work with and lead are affected by how we live our convictions. It takes conviction to keep agreements and follow through on those agreements or renegotiate when we are honestly unable to meet them. It takes conviction to be consistent in our behavior and to be in harmony with our personal values as well as the organization's. And it takes conviction to speak up and confront behavior that we know undermines trust in our relationships.

Are we authentic in our words and actions? Unfortunately, in many work environments, authenticity is punished. So what happens? People go underground with the truth, become inauthentic in their words and actions—they betray themselves. Trust in ourselves and in others diminishes.

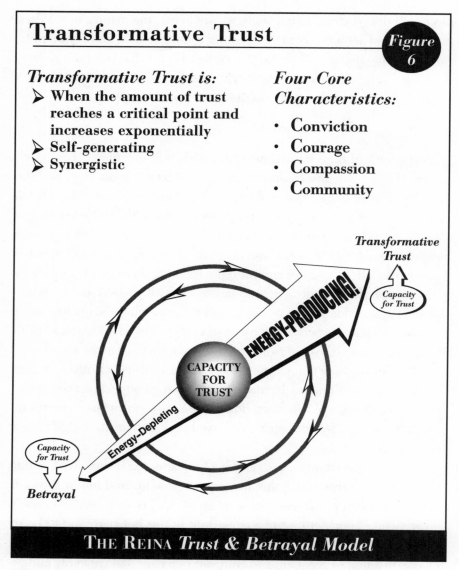

Figure 6   Transformative Trust

Living by our convictions every day is hard work. It takes discipline, focus, energy, and effort. Yet it is through daily discipline that we achieve confidence and competence and expand our capacity for trust.

Leaders who are clear about their convictions are in a position to help others arrive at the same level of clarity within themselves. Others become empowered. The result is an expanded capacity for trust in self and others.

Courage

Courage comes from the French word *coeur,* which means "heart." In our hearts is the truth we can trust.[1] Yet it takes courage to trust it and to do what we know is right. We must be willing to take action in tough situations in spite of the potential consequences.

It takes courage to let go of the need for control and delegate greater responsibilities to your employees—responsibilities that you enjoy and take pride and pleasure in doing and for which you remain accountable. But to help employees learn and grow, you know you must demonstrate your trust in their competence.

It takes courage to be true to your values: to speak up and point out a betrayal resulting from the organization's not practicing the values it espouses, to point out lapses of integrity or disservices to people at work and to take the lead in correcting them.

It takes courage to tell the truth in the face of adversity and not put a spin on it: to tell employees that things are tough, that the company just lost a major portion of its business to an offshore operation and may have to lay people off, some who have been working at the plant most of their adult lives, or that the company has just been sold to a larger firm and that there will be major restructuring. It takes courage to speak from the heart, to share that this is a painful time for you, that you deeply care about your people and don't want to let them down, yet you just don't know what will happen.

Leaders have a rich opportunity to provide a deeper understanding of relationships at work, to recognize betrayal and participate in the renewal of trust. It takes courage to recognize betrayal and to take the first step to heal broken trust and mend relationships. When we do this, we honor our relationship with ourselves and with others. When we don't, we perpetrate yet another betrayal—of ourselves and of the potential in the relationship.

Betrayal can be a gift and a teacher, if we allow ourselves to receive it and embrace the learning it offers.

Compassion

Do employees know you care about them? As leaders attempting to navigate change in your organizations, do you have the compassion to acknowledge the uncertainty, confusion, vulnerability, and pain that you feel and that your employees must feel? Do you remain sensitive to how your actions affect others? This level of relating produces the very type of climate organizations are attempting to create, one that is flexible and adaptable.

Through a sense of community, the level of trust between people is so strong that they no longer rely on the traditional ways of conducting business. For instance, people are not as inclined to rely on a formal contract. "In fact, operating strictly by the contract impedes performance," the division manager of a telecommunications company noted. Compassion gives people awareness and understanding for others. Operating from this awareness enhances the individuals' capacity for trust and the organization's. Relationships are strengthened.

When compassion exists, people feel safe to communicate at a deeper level of honesty. There is a freer exchange of feedback with the underlying interest of helping one another develop. It takes compassion to receive feedback in a constructive way—to appreciate the intentions of the other party, to listen actively, to put our defenses aside in an effort to take in and understand what is being offered.

It takes compassion to have honest conversations, particularly when we have been hurt and are being asked to forgive the one who hurt us. When we are able to look beyond our own pain and stop blaming others for their shortcomings, we release energy in a way that opens the door to forgiveness.[2] We become lighter. Trust begins to grow.

We used to think that forgiveness was about giving the other person a break. We are learning it is more about freeing oneself from the burden of distrust, freeing the energy within oneself from blame, from holding onto the notion that someone else is responsible for the bad things that happen to us.

The act of forgiveness is an act of creation in itself. It is the process of letting go that frees up our energy for more productive purposes. Forgiveness gives the rebuilding of trust permission to begin. As such, trust is an act of creation. By making the first move to rebuild a relationship, by extending trust, we create trust. By being willing to forgive others who have broken trust with us, we begin to rebuild the relationship. We are not talking about naively forgiving or granting blind trust here. We may forgive the person, but we might not forget the behavior that broke the trust.

At the transformative level of trust, employees have compassion for one another. They are able to walk in their coworkers' shoes. They realize that at any moment in time, people are probably doing the absolute best they can do, even though we sense that we might have done it better. Compassion is understanding that given the opportunity, people want to contribute, want to make a difference, if we allow them to do so.

Community

Where there is transformative trust, leaders take an active role in helping people see that they are part of a larger whole. People see the underlying meaning in what they do and their contribution to the larger system. At the transformative level of trust, a shared vision is the binding force that aligns people and provides a sense of community. The vision is lived and supported every day through actions.

When people feel connected through a foundation of trust, they automatically cooperate with one another. They take responsibility and honor their agreements in the spirit of relationship. People feel secure counting on one another to get the job done. Through their connection with one another, people shift their focus of operating from "I" to "we." Trust grows.

At the transformative level of trust, the workplace community promotes a level of openness and honesty. People feel safe to discuss deeper issues of interest and matters of importance to them. People willingly admit mistakes and mention errors to be corrected because they know not doing so would be a betrayal to their community. People feel free to ask for help without fear of looking incompetent in the eyes of their leader or coworkers. In their connection to their workplace community, people recognize and act on the opportunity to give and take, learn and teach, help and be helped.

At the transformative level of trust, leaders invest in their community. They know that the only way to achieve the organization's objectives is through the collective knowledge and experience of the community. Leaders support their people in expressing deeper aspects of themselves while pursuing the organization's business objectives. Leaders create conditions where people can thrive. The behaviors of transactional trust and transformative trust are integrated. Relationships experience a renewal of trust that enables people to unleash their vast creative and productive energies (see Figure 7).

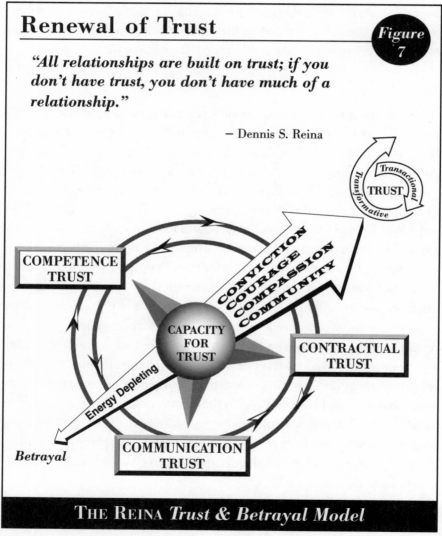

Renewal of Trust

Figure 7

"All relationships are built on trust; if you don't have trust, you don't have much of a relationship."

— Dennis S. Reina

TRANSACTIONAL / TRANSFORMATIVE — TRUST

CONVICTION
COURAGE
COMPASSION
COMMUNITY

COMPETENCE TRUST

CAPACITY FOR TRUST

CONTRACTUAL TRUST

Energy Depleting

COMMUNICATION TRUST

Betrayal

THE REINA *Trust & Betrayal Model*

Figure 7   Renewal of Trust

CONCLUSION

We do not know what the future holds for organizations; we can only anticipate the challenges we face and do our best to prepare for them. We do know, however, that regardless of what the future holds, it will take people to make it happen. And people, regardless of where they work or what they do, want very much the same thing: trust in their relationships.

Are we willing to be catalysts for transforming the quality of relationships between leaders and employees, among teams, and across departments in our organizations? Are we willing to establish work environments where people are excited about what they are doing and with whom they are working? Are we willing to create organizational communities where people have an opportunity to express who they are and to be fully present at work? Are we up for the challenge?

Leaders have the opportunity to develop trust at work, and their people are looking to them to take the first step. This is not easy work. However, the Reina Trust & Betrayal Model provides a framework for beginning. By trusting in ourselves and choosing to trust in others, we begin the journey.

IDEAS IN ACTION

Here we examine what leaders can do to begin moving their organizations toward transformative trust. The questions may be used for self-reflection or to coach other individuals in their growth and development.

Using the Four Core Characteristics to Transform Your Organization

1. At work, where do you see evidence of conviction?
    a. Aside from receiving a paycheck, why do you work?
    b. What higher purpose does your work serve?
    c. How can we create a more meaningful work environment within our team, our department, our company?
    d. What values and principles will strengthen our capacity to trust in ourselves, our teammates, our department, and our company?

    e. How can we improve the way we live by those values and principles?

2. What behaviors on the job reflect courage?

    a. What is an example of a courageous act that would enhance trust or transform the level of trust within our team?

    b. What is an example of a courageous act that would enhance trust or transform the level of trust within our company or department?

    c. Express the unexpressed. What should be said or done that isn't being said or done?

3. What forms does compassion take on the job?

    a What are examples of compassion that would enhance trust within the team? Across the organization?

    b. What do we need to do to forgive ourselves or others within our team, department, or company?

4. At work, where do you see evidence of a sense of community?

    a. What does being accountable for the whole team or organization mean on an everyday on-the-job basis?

    b. In what ways or areas do we need to be more accountable to the team?

    c. What does being accountable for our unit, department, or organization mean on an everyday on-the-job basis? In what areas or ways do we need to be more accountable? To our unit? To our department? To our entire organization?

REFERENCES

CHAPTER 1

1. C. Lee, "Trust Me," *Training Magazine,* January 1997, p. 30.
2. J. Amodeo, *Love and Betrayal: Broken Trust in Intimate Relationships* (New York: Ballantine Books, 1994), p. 11.

CHAPTER 2

1. K. Griffin and R. E. Barnes, *Trusting Me, Trusting You* (Columbus, Ohio: Merrill, 1973).
2. J. Rotter, "Interpersonal Trust, Trustworthiness, and Gullibility," *American Psychologist 35* (1980): 1–7.
3. Ibid.
4. Ibid., p. 6.
5. E. Erikson, *Childhood and Society* (New York: Norton, 1950).
6. D. Tway and L. Davis, "Leadership as Trustbuilding: Communication and Trust." In *Eighth Annual Texas Conference on Organizations* (Austin: University of Texas, 1993), pp. 48–52.
7. D. Brothers, *Falling Backwards: An Exploration of Trust and Self-Experience* (New York: Norton, 1995).

CHAPTER 3

1. Brothers, *Falling Backwards.* What Brothers called *realism,* we are calling *pragmatism.*
2. Ibid.
3. R. van Oech, *A Whack on the Side of the Head* (New York: Harper & Row, 1984).

CHAPTER 4

1. B. Hedva, *Journey from Betrayal to Trust: A Universal Rite of Passage* (Berkeley, Calif.: Celestial Arts, 1992), p. 7.
2. J. Hillman, *Loose Ends: Primary Papers in Archetypal Psychology* (Dallas, Texas: Spring, 1975); ibid., p. 9.

3. G. Mellinger, "Interpersonal Trust as a Factor in Communications," *Journal of Abnormal and Social Psychology,* 52 (1956): 304.
4. Amodeo, *Love and Betrayal,* p. 43.

CHAPTER 5

1. Amodeo, *Love and Betrayal,* p. 43.
2. Hillman, *Loose Ends,* p. 67.
3. E. Kübler-Ross, *Death: The Final Stage of Growth* (Englewood Cliffs, N.J.: Prentice Hall, 1975).
4. R. D. Carson, *Taming Your Gremlin: A Guide to Enjoying Yourself* (New York: Harper & Row, 1986).
5. Hedva, *Journey from Betrayal to Trust,* p. 16.
6. Ibid., p. 20.
7. L. B. Smedes, *Forgive and Forget: Healing the Hurts We Don't Deserve* (San Francisco: HarperSanFrancisco, 1996).
8. Ibid.
9. Ibid.
10. Hedva, *Journey from Betrayal to Trust,* p. 19.

CHAPTER 6

1. J. Billings, "A Study of Nonverbal Behaviors of School Principals and Their Relationships to the Principals' Ability to Develop Trust and to Motivate Staffs," doctoral dissertation, Claremont Graduate School, 1988; B. Nanus, "Doing the Right Thing," *Bureaucrat,* Fall 1986, pp. 9–12; W. Bennis and B. Nanus, *Leaders: The Strategies for Taking Charge* (New York: Harper & Row, 1984); K. Roberts and C. O'Reilly, "Measuring Organizational Communication," *Journal of Applied Psychology,* 59 (1974): 321–326; J. Rotter, "A New Scale for the Measurement of Interpersonal Trust," *Journal of Personality,* 35 (1967): 651–655.
2. W. E. Baker, *Networking Smart: How to Build Relationships for Personal and Organizational Success* (New York: McGraw-Hill, 1994), p. 38.
3. Ibid., p. 83.
4. F. Friedlander, "The Ecology of Work Groups." In *Handbook of Organizational Behavior,* ed. E. J. Lorsch (Englewood Cliffs, N.J.: Prentice Hall, 1970).
5. R. Swinth, "The Establishment of the Trust Relationship," *Journal of Conflict Resolution,* 11 (1967): 335–337.
6. G. Lippitt, *Organizational Renewal* (Englewood Cliffs, N.J.: Prentice Hall, 1982).
7. R. W. Rogers, *The Psychological Contract of Trust: Trust Development in the '90s Workplace* (Pittsburgh, Pa.: Development Dimensions International, 1994), p. 32.
8. R. B. Shaw, *Trust in the Balance: Building Successful Organizations on Results, Integrity, and Concern* (San Francisco: Jossey-Bass, 1997), p. 32.
9. Ibid., p. 66.

CHAPTER 7

1. A. Bruzzese, "Open Books," *Human Resource Executive,* May 1990, pp. 49–50.
2. J. Patterson, "Fundamentals of Leadership," *ASTD pamphlet,* 1994): p. 5.
3. G. Bell, *Getting Things Done When You Are Not in Charge* (San Francisco: Jossey-Bass, 1994).
4. F. J. Navran, *Truth and Trust: The First Two Victims of Downsizing* (Athabasca, Alberta, Canada: Athabasca Educational University Enterprises, 1995), p. 132.
5. Ibid, p. 132.
6. G. M. Parker, *Team Players and Teamwork: The New Competitive Business Strategy* (San Francisco: Jossey-Bass, 1990), p. 47.
7. P. B. Kritek, *Negotiating at an Uneven Table: Developing Moral Courage in Resolving Our Conflicts* (San Francisco: Jossey-Bass, 1994), p. 210.
8. Dr. Leslie Faerstein quoted in J. Wackenhut and A. Weinberger, "Truth About Lying," *New York,* December 1983, p. 47.
9. M. Landesberg, *The Tao of Coaching: Boost Your Effectiveness at Work by Inspiring Those Around You* (Santa Monica, Calif.: Knowledge Exchange, 1997).
10. Baker, *Networking Smart,* p. 47.
11. D. McGregor, *The Professional Manager* (New York: McGraw-Hill, 1967), p. 163.

CHAPTER 8

1. R. D. White, "Motivation Reconsidered: The Concept of Competence," *Psychological Review, 66* (1959): 297–333.
2. J. Whitney, *The Economics of Trust* (New York: McGraw-Hill, 1994), p. 125.
3. Ibid., pp. 125–126.
4. D. Goleman, *Emotional Intelligence* (New York: Bantam Books, 1995).
5. N. Tichy and S. Sherman, "Jack Welch's Lessons for Success," *Fortune Magazine,* January 25, 1993, p. 29.
6. Ibid, p. 26.
7. R. Grossman, "Damaged, Downsized Souls," *HR Magazine,* May 1996, pp. 54–62.
8. P. B. Vaill, *Learning as a Way of Being: Strategies for Survival in a World of Permanent White Water* (San Francisco: Jossey-Bass, 1996).

CHAPTER 9

1. Adapted from R. Napier and M. Gershenfeld, *Groups: Theory and Experience,* 5th ed. (Boston: Houghton Mifflin, 1993).
2. Rogers, *The Psychological Contract of Trust,* p. 41–42.
3. J. R. Katzenbach and D. K. Smith, *The Wisdom of Teams: Creating the High-Performance Organization* (Boston: Harvard Business School Press, 1993).

CHAPTER 10

1. R. Nelson, "The Care of the Un-Downsized," *Training and Development*, April, 1997, p. 42.
2. Navran, *Truth and Trust*, p. 133.
3. Hedva, *Journey from Betrayal to Trust*, p. 16.
4. Navran, *Truth and Trust*, p. 134.
5. Ibid, p. 132.
6. J. M. Kouzes and B. Z. Posner, *Credibility: How Leaders Gain and Lose It, Why People Demand It* (San Francisco: Jossey-Bass, 1996), p. 110.

CHAPTER 11

1. Hedva, *Journey from Betrayal to Trust*, p. 5.
2. Smedes, *Forgive and Forget*, p. 224.

INDEX

ABOUT THE AUTHORS

Dennis S. Reina and Michelle L. Reina are devoted to working with organizations that want to build trust in the workplace and with leaders who want a capable workforce. They are principles of the organization development research and consulting firm, Chagnon & Reina Associates, Inc., based in Stowe, Vermont.

Experienced in system-wide change efforts, team development, and one-on-one coaching, Dennis and Michelle provide organizations with a variety of practical tools, resources, and instruments that help people at all levels develop a common language and a shared understanding of trust. They help leaders increase the level of trust among their people to produce healthy relationships in the workplace and become high-performing organizations.

Dennis and Michelle's interest in trust began through their work facilitating change and developing teams in organizations. They saw that trust was the critical factor in the success or failure of these change efforts. In addition, they have observed the strong desire people have to understand and experience trust in workplace relationships.

The Reinas have presented their work at conferences throughout the country and have been guest lecturers at colleges and universities. Additionally, they have written for a variety of publications and appeared on numerous radio programs. They are considered leading authorities on trust-related issues in the workplace.

Dennis has masters degrees in Organizational Development and Holistic Health Education and earned his Ph.D. in Human and Organizational Systems from the Fielding Institute in Santa Barbara, California. Michelle earned her master's degree in Organizational Development and a Ph.D. in Human and Organizational systems from the Fielding Institute. Through their years of pioneering research, Dennis and Michelle have worked with such companies as AT&T, BFGoodrich Aerospace, Harvard University, Ben & Jerry's Homemade Inc., Bankers Trust, Walt Disney World, Fletcher Allen Health Care, and Wyeth Nutritionals.

Dennis, Michelle, and their two sons, Patrick and William, live in Stowe, Vermont. They try to find enough time for each other and their interests. As a family, they enjoy hiking, canoeing, skiing, biking, swimming, music, dancing and spending time together.

Chagnon & Reina Associates, Inc. Trust-Building Resources

The following supporting materials are currently available to assist you in building trust in your organization:

- **The Reina Trust & Betrayal Model**™
  An easy-to-understand practical framework that illustrates the complex dynamics of trust and betrayal in the workplace relationships.

- **The Reina Introduction to Building Trust in the Workplace Program**
  An interactive training program designed to introduce participants to The Reina Trust & Betrayal Model, to provide a common language to discuss and take action on trust-related issues.

- **The Reina Building Trust in the Workplace Certification Program**
  A multi-day certification workshop designed to provide Human Resource or Organizational Development professionals with an understanding of the complex dynamics of trust and betrayal in the workplace using the Reina Trust & Betrayal Model™. This program qualifies participants to administer the Reina Organizational Trust Scale™, the Reina Team Trust Scale™, and the Reina Trust in Leadership Scale™.

- **The Trust & Betrayal in the Workplace Video**
  An engaging and informative training video that captures key elements from this book which facilitates active dialogue regarding trust related issues in the workplace.

To learn more about these trust building resources, consulting and coaching services, and instrumentation to measure trust in your organization or team, please contact us.

Building Trust in Your Organization: Your Stories and Questions

We would like to hear your stories about trust and betrayal in your organization. Tell us about your relationships at work. Tell us about your painful experiences of betrayal. Share with us your positive experiences of building or rebuilding trust in your relationships at work. What worked, what did not? What powerful lessons did you learn?

Are there questions you have regarding trust and betrayal or other related areas about our work? Let us know if you need more information.

We hope you received value from reading about the experiences in this book. We look forward to hearing from you and can be reached at:

Chagnon & Reina Associates, Inc.
560 Black Bear Run, Stowe, VT 05672
phone: (802)253-8808
fax: (802)253-8818
email: dsreina@trustinworkplace.com
            mlreina@trustinworkplace.com
website: www:trustinworkplace.com